SWEENEY

THE DEMON BARBER O

by

C. G. BOND

SAMUEL FRENCH

LONDON
NEW YORK   TORONTO   SYDNEY   HOLLYWOOD

Please see page vi for further copyright information

SWEENEY TODD

by the

DIRECTOR

The Majority of Thriller/Melodramas, of which *Sweeney Todd* has always been one of the best-known, were written and performed with the express purpose of providing audiences with the thrills, horror and shocks which they have always, traditionally, enjoyed. In recent years, however, the seemingly endless stream of Horror films produced by, in some cases, very brilliant film-makers, have explored every conceivable means of doing this, and with far greater impact and realism than could ever be achieved in the Theatre.

The Theatre's answer to this has been to present plays of this type as an opportunity for the cast and director to indulge in a jolly romp, "hamming" the passion, and sending-up the romance and pathos. Snarling, leering villains, behind-the-hand asides, posturing heroes and swooning heroines are all exaggerated to the extreme, and thus, in presenting a play in this way, one is merely inviting the audience to join in the fun and laugh at this comment on what is, in most cases, a rather superficial and crudely constructed play about one-dimensional characters with whom the audience must find great difficulty in identifying.

When I first read this version by C. G. Bond, I was immediately aware of the fact that he had written, not only an entirely new play based on the original idea, but one with a real plot, characters, genuine comedy situations and, above all, something to say. It struck me as a very positive comment on the fact that we have come to accept such things as violence, wholesale murder—and worse—as part of our everyday lives. The love scene between Todd and Mrs Lovett, played over a bowl containing "black-pudding-mix" (the ingredients are, of course, of human origin), is terrifying in its domestic normality, but are we really so very far away from this ourselves?

There was never any doubt in my mind about the style in which I would direct the play. The production, I decided, would be absolutely "straight". The sets, costumes and props must all be authentic, not least of which "The Chair" would have to be totally convincing. The cast would play for the truth of the situations, and leave the strength of the play—its drama, horror and comedy—to take care of itself. In the true style of melodrama, however, the actors would be encouraged to express their emotions freely and fully, with truth, but without "over-acting". In all the earlier versions of this play, the central character of Sweeney Todd has always been written and portrayed as a homicidal maniac, murdering his customers in order to rob them, and forcing others, through fear, to share in his crimes, but there has never been any explanation or justification for this. In C. G. Bond's version, however, Todd starts out as a sympathetic character. An ordinary man whose initial motive is one of revenge for the wrongs committed against him and his family, but who soon succumbs to the fascination of holding the power of life or death in his hands. I decided, therefore, that Todd should be played as normally and sanely as possible within the context of the play, and this interpretation was responsible for emphasizing the horror of the situation. The response from the audiences was extraordinary. Schoolchildren, locals, intellectuals and critics alike were unanimous in praising the fact that it was performed absolutely "straight", and that they were thus completely involved in the play from start to finish. Several parties of schoolchildren came back more than once to see the production, as did many members of the local community, and it was also interesting to note that there were sometimes parties of people who had come simply to have a good time hissing the villains and cheering the heroes, who would start off doing so indiscriminately, but after a while would become so involved in the play that their participation was completely spontaneous. To sit amongst an audience shouting out to the heroine, "Don't sit in the chair!" with *genuine* concern was, for me, a most exciting experience, but in fact, the production was not designed specifically for audience participation (although this is normally the policy of the theatre in which it was performed) and yet the response, as far as this aspect was concerned, was more positive than anything previously experienced.

MAXWELL SHAW

SWEENEY TODD

by the

AUTHOR

There have been at least six versions of *Sweeney Todd, the Demon Barber of Fleet Street* since George Dibdin-Pitt's original melodrama was first performed in 1847 at The Brittania, a London "Bloodbath" (a theatre devoted almost exclusively to melodramas). Nor was Pitt's play entirely original, he based it on a "penny dreadful", a newsheet containing sensational descriptions of depravity violence and grotesque murder with a few lines of pious editorial humbug at the end—the mixture is still on sale every Sunday, just as dreadful but now it costs ten or eleven times the original penny. Where the "penny dreadful" got its "facts" from nobody knows, although there was a Jacobin barber in Paris during the French Revolution who achieved the difficult feat (under the prevailing circumstances) of shocking the public by perpetrating a series of bizarre murders upon his clients: but there the similarity ends: no trick chair, and no Mrs Lovett's meat pies, these belong to the "penny dreadful". All the versions of the play have contained the chair and the pies, and so does mine—I would hardly have the temerity to call my play *Sweeney Todd* if it didn't. However, I've cast my net wider than anyone else in "borrowing" from other authors: I make no apology for this, after all, as the man himself said: "A beggar may eat of a fish that hath fed of a worm that hath ate of a King." I have "borrowed" from, amongst others, *The Count of Monte Christo, The Revenger's Tragedy, The Spanish Tragedy*, the family greengrocer, and Shakespeare, as well as Dibdin-Pitt's original melodrama. My object has been to add to the chair and the pies an exciting story, characters that are large but real, and situations that, given a mad world not unlike our own, are believable. For these seem to me to be the ingredients that melodrama has lost in recent years; undoubtedly in its heyday during the last century melodrama involved people, entertained them, frightened, amused and moved them: nowadays the fashion is to "send them up", and ask the audience merely to laugh at the *naïveté* of their forbears. This seems to me a pity, and I have tried to add to the original idea of melodrama to make it more acceptable to a modern audience.

I enjoyed writing this *Sweeney Todd* and I hope you enjoy reading and/or performing it—because that is the key to making it work!

C. G. BOND

SWEENEY TODD

First presented by the Theatre Workshop at the Theatre Royal, Stratford, London, with the following cast of characters:

Anthony Hope	Brian Protheroe
Sweeney Todd	Brian Murphy
A Beggar Woman	Paola Dionisotti
Mrs Lovett, of the Pie Shop	Avis Bunnage
A Beadle	Ken Hill
Judge Turpin	Ron Hackett
Tobias Ragg	Tom Owen
A Balding Man	Trevor T. Smith
Alfredo Pirelli	John Lyons
Johanna	Lorna Heilbron
Jonas Fogg	Trevor T. Smith

The play directed by Maxwell Shaw

Setting by Tony Woollard

The action of the play passes in the City of London

Time – early nineteenth century

ACT I

SCENE 1

Fleet Street. Night

A Lamplighter crosses, then a young couple. A Beggar Woman follows. Anthony Hope and Sweeney Todd enter

Anthony I have sailed the world, beheld its fairest cities, seen the pyramids, the wonders of the east. Yet it is true—there *is* no place like home.

Todd None.

Anthony What's the matter?

Todd You are young. Life has been kind to you, and fortune smiles on your enterprises. May it always be so. My heart beats quicker, too, to find myself in London once again, but whether out of joy or fear I cannot say.

The Beggar Woman approaches them

Beggar Woman Alms! (*She holds out her bowl*) Help a poor unfortunate woman. Mister?

Anthony (*giving her a coin*) Here, go in peace.

Beggar Woman God bless you! (*To Todd*) And you, sir? Will you not have mercy on a . . .

Todd Be off with you. Leave us.

She stares at him. He turns away

Beggar Woman Your—face! (*She tries to move round him*) There's something—I . . .

Todd I said be off! Deluded hag! (*He goes to strike her*)

The Beggar Woman scuttles off

Todd sees Anthony watching him. He recovers himself

Anthony My friend, I have honoured the promise I made you at the start of our long journey, and never once have I questioned you. But now my curiosity overwhelms me. Why do you hide your face? What can frighten you in a poor beggar like that?

Todd (*abstractedly*) I thought it impossible that anyone should recognize me.

Anthony She did not. She is mad. But why should you fear if she did?

Todd I owe my life to you, Anthony. Without you and your good ship I would be long dead, so perhaps I owe it to you to tell you the truth. I, too, have sailed across the world, but I have seen no wonders—unless the angry noonday sun, shrivelling a man's shadow to a smudge beneath his feet, be a wonder. Or the greed and cruelty that forces a man to fight his own brother to the death for a crust of bread. Such "wonders" as these I have seen—and worse that I will not relate, for you could not believe it. When you found me clinging to my makeshift raft, half mad with thirst, you found a man devoid of hope—an escaped prisoner whose desperation made him dare his captors and the elements to seek his freedom in the jaws of certain death.

Anthony What was your crime?

Todd My wife was beautiful.

Anthony Why, if that be a crime . . .

Todd A heinous one in this same town you call home. For here there are men who cannot look on beauty, and not defile it: who scratch and tear at virtue's shining face with fumbling hands till they have made it ugly as their own. Two such men there were—two upright men —a beadle and a judge, who tried with every flattery, every temptation, to win my wife to their desires. But she, bright angel, would have none of them. So—then they worked their devilish practices. Falsely, I was charged with petty theft, arrested—by the beadle, and brought straight to court before that same judge, who, in accents grave, sentenced me to transportation for life, hoping that in my absence my good wife would fall.

Anthony And did she?

Todd No! (*Helplessly*) I do not know. That is what I hope to find out— here. My barber's shop was in the upper storey, but as you see—a barber's shop no more. Here, below, lives Mrs Lovett. I hope she will have news for me. Now leave me, Anthony, to learn my fate. I would not have you see me weep—whether for joy or sorrow.

Anthony I will. Shall we meet tomorrow?

Todd Yes. At St Dunstan's market-place. At noon.

Anthony I will be there. Farewell. I'll pray for your good fortune.

Anthony goes

Todd Farewell, my friend. A wife and daughter left behind in deadly peril, unprotected. What spite befell them? The answer lies within. Yet I must not be known to anyone I cannot trust. Well. I have no choice— my fate awaits me.

Todd enters the pie shop

Music. The Lights change

SCENE 2

Mrs Lovett's pieshop

Todd enters

Todd (*calling*) Are you all asleep? Some food, here.

Mrs Lovett enters

Mrs Lovett Are you a ghost?

Todd starts for the door, fearing he has been recognized

Hey, don't go running out the minute you get in. I only took you for a ghost 'cos you're the first customer I've seen for a fortnight. Sit you down.

Todd sits, warily

You'd think we had the plague, the way people avoid this shop. A pie, was it?

Todd A pie—yes. And some ale.

Mrs Lovett (*getting the pie*) Mind you, you can't hardly blame them. There's no denying these are the most tasteless pies in London. I should know, I make 'em. (*She puts the pie on the table, then flicks a bit of dirt off the crust*) Ugh! What's that? But can you wonder, with meat the price it is? I mean, I never thought I'd see the day when grown men and good cooks, too, would dribble over a dead dog like it was a round of beef. (*She goes for some ale*)

Todd I hardly wonder your trade's bad if you talk like this to all your customers.

Mrs Lovett (*bringing the jug and tankard to the table*) Well, sir, I speaks as finds, I do. And what I'm telling you is the plain and simple truth. Mind you, they do say necessity's the mother of invention. The other day, Tuesday it was, I was walking down Cheapside, and I saw a crowd of people looking in a pie shop window. Well, I thought, I'd better have a look an' all. And there in the window, pretty as a picture, was a roasted cat all garnished round with little mice tied up to look like sausages. Beautiful it was. But how am I to catch mice, with me legs like what they are? Not to mention me wind. Oh, times is very hard.

Todd Yes. (*After a pause*) Don't the family that live above pay you any rent?

Mrs Lovett No, there's no-one lives up there, sir. Been empty for years. There was a barber and his family that lived there once—ooh, a lovely man, he was, a *real* man, but he got transported across the seas. Mind you, he deserved it.

Todd Deserved it! What was his crime?

Mrs Lovett Foolishness. Mind you his wife didn't help much. She was a brainless creature. Two proper gentlemen took a fancy to her, you see, but she wouldn't have none of it, and her husband, poor fool, instead of fetching her one round the mouth and leaving his bed for a couple of nights—he encouraged these fancy notions in her. Well—daft, weren't it? I would have had him down here for a couple of nights—and more if he'd wanted. But no, he had to make a song and dance of it. Well, stands to reason, they shipped him off.

Todd What became of his wife? And were there no children?

Mrs Lovett There was a daughter, yes. Both cried themselves silly, they did, when he'd gone.

During Mrs Lovett's narration of the following events a dumb show is performed of them. It opens with Mrs Todd and Johanna weeping. Beadle, Judge and Onlookers enter and join in as described

Then one day Beadle came to call on her—to try his luck, you see—but she wasn't having any. Then he says as how the Judge had repented of himself and wanted to try and help get her husband back. And she, poor soul believed him. Beadle said as how the Judge had taken to his bed in a terrible state and would she come to the Inns of Court that night to see what could be done for her poor husband. Well, she went, but when she got there they was having this fancy dress ball, you see, all in masks, they was, and she didn't know what to do, couldn't find the Judge anywhere. But he found her soon enough, and he were in a terrible state all right—but it weren't with repentance or nothing like that. She tried to fight him off, but the Beadle helped like, and what could she do on her own? All of them at the ball just looked on, you see. Watched, like.

By this time Mrs Todd, surrounded by onlookers, is being raped by the Judge. Sweeney Todd can bear it no longer

Todd Will no-one have mercy on her?

The onlookers laugh as the dumb show dissolves

Then I will have no mercy either. None.

Mrs Lovett Here, you are in a state. You've hardly touched your pie.

Todd (*seizing Mrs Lovett and forcing her to look closely at him*) I am that poor unfortunate woman's husband: that foolish barber so unjustly transported. Now tell me, woman, what became of my wife and daughter?

Mrs Lovett You *are* him! But how you've changed. You look as if you've shook hands with the devil and come back to tell it.

Todd Where is my wife? My Lucy?

Mrs Lovett Oh, sir . . .

Todd Where is she?

Mrs Lovett When she came back here she were in a pitiful state. Her hair was all across her face and her eyes were all wild like an animal's. She went straight up where Johanna was sleeping and woke her up. Then she gave the poor mite poison and took the rest herself.

Sweeney Todd falls to the ground

Oh now, don't distress yourself so. Yer can't bring 'em back that way, you know. (*Kneeling beside him*) There, there, you haven't changed much, have you? Still as soft as butter.

She cradles his head until he is somewhat recovered

Todd Oh, you shall see a change in me. That husband, soft as butter, died on that same night. And in his place shall rise such a man to put the world to fright, and this I vow, I will not rest until my wife and daughter be avenged.

Mrs Lovett No, no, you didn't let me finish. It was just your wife that died.

Todd Johanna lives?

Mrs Lovett As surely as I do—and pretty as a picture, too. I revived the poor mite, sat up with her three nights when she couldn't take no nourishment down at all, but after that she got stronger and in next to no time she was good as new.

Todd (*making to search for her*) Where is she? Let me see her.

Mrs Lovett Oh, she's not here. I couldn't keep her.

Todd Where is she, then?

Mrs Lovett The Judge came looking for her when he heard as how your wife was dead. He weren't happy about it, you see, after he'd got what he wanted. Said he'd set her up in the world, and took her off of me— to be his ward, he said.

Todd He shall pay dearly. This do I vow, this heart shall be as stone. These hands of mine shall drip with guilty blood: this face strike cowards dead as look on it. I will be revenged.

Mrs Lovett But how can yer be? He's a judge, the other's a beadle, and you're a poor penniless escaped convict, running from the law. How can yer be revenged on 'em?

Todd Some way. Any way. I will have blood. But you are right, the plan I have in mind requires money. If only I had my razors I know where I might find some.

Mrs Lovett Oh, Mr . . .

Todd Todd, Sweeney Todd. The other man is dead.

Mrs Lovett Oh, all right, "Mr Todd". Here's a crumb of comfort for you. (*She goes and gets the razors in a box and brings them back to him*) I found your razors upstairs when I was clearing out—to pay for the funeral, like. But I thought I'd hang on to them. (*She makes up to him*) I remembered how you treasured them, you see, and I always had a fondness for you and hoped you might come back one day and . . . Well, never mind that for the present. But here they are, shining like they was new. I was offered a hundred pounds for them, I was, and in my position, well—(*she examines them lovingly*)—I was tempted, but I didn't fall.

Todd (*taking a razor from the box*) My right hand is complete again.

Mrs Lovett Them handles is chased silver, ain't they?

Todd Silver—yes!

Mrs Lovett See how they shine.

Todd Aye, but before too long this blade will make its handle seem as dull as common lead. For from its edge shall drip inestimable rubies.

SCENE 3

St Dunstan's Market-Place

Tobias Ragg is discovered, together with shoppers, street vendors, the Beadle, and the Beggar Woman

Tobias Gentlemen! Gentlemen! Your attention per-lease. Have you seen cripples throw away their crutches? Heard dumb men speak? Seen dead men rise from out the ground and caper round the town? Well? Have you? Have you seen life spring anew where once it was extinct? If you have seen these things, then go about your business. For I have nothing new to tell you. But if you would behold a miracle—here, in this very square, then stay and hearken. For I have seen death's dreadful tread averted, seen precious life burgeon from barren soil. I have seen this and touched it with these trembling hands. Here. On the top of my head.

Sweeney Todd enters during the final words of the above

(*Catching his breath and staring above the heads of the onlookers as if he has seen a ghost*) O! My mother, mother. (*He stretches out his hands as if to touch someone*) Gone, gone. Your pardon, gentlemen, methought I saw my mother—oh, so pale, so pale—she who first suckled me and from whose breast I learnt that truth is golden and that liars go to hell, but 'tis impossible. Ah, gentlemen, when I was but a lad of seven years old, death rudely snatched her from me, and I, a lad who knew no other comfort but her yielding bosom, was thrust into the workhouse. This change was almost mortal to me. I wasted down to nothing, could not eat, nor sleep, scarce breathe . . .

Beadle Now then, young feller, there's nothing wrong with the workhouse. I take an interest in the lads myself.

Tobias No, no, you miss my meaning, sir, The workhouse was a warm and happy place. It was my mother's death that made me so ill. (*Searching for his lines again*) That it was that made me—er—was almost mortal to me. I wasted down to nothing, could not eat nor sleep, scarce breathe. And all my hair fell out. Upon my honour, it is true. I had no more hair on my head than an egg. Oh, I was in a terrible state. But, gentlemen, here is the miracle. A barber-surgeon found me in this wretched plight, and where all the kindness of the workhouse people failed—his ministrations saved me. He gave me a bottle of a substance rare as gold—Pirelli's Miracle Elixir—and rubbed it in with loving fingers thrice a day. Behold my head! There lies the miracle! New life grows there, new hope, new strength. Now who will take advantage of this miracle? Who needs new life? You, sir? And you?

Two gentlemen come forward, one with receding hair

For only tuppence you can be as me. Here, feel its strength . . .

While Tobias is selling the hair restorer Anthony Hope enters, looking for Sweeney Todd

Anthony Ah, there you are, my friend. I'm sorry to have kept you waiting, but . . .
Todd Sssh! Listen, I may need your help. And the favour I ask may be a painful one.
Anthony You could not cause me pain today.
Todd Then I may count on you?
Anthony Of course.
Tobias Are you all done for the Pirelli's Miracle Elixir? Right. Then who will step inside and have a shave from the Prince of Barbers, the man who shaved the King of Naples before the Battle of Pistolero and to whom, you will recall, the King dedicated that glorious victory? Or who will have the raging toothache assuaged by the man who pulled a tooth out from a Medici princess's mouth so skilfully she thought he'd kissed her, so she swooned and asked for more? The man who, every week, to back his claims, offers a challenge to the world? He will wager one hundred pounds that he can shave a man and pull out one of his teeth, with no more pain than a pin-prick, faster than any barber-surgeon in the land. Who will be shaved by such a man? Who'll have a troublesome tooth so gently drawn they'll smile as it comes out?
Todd Pwaaugh! What a stench! Is there a charnel house near by?
Beadle There's nothing wrong with the drains round here, mate—I've seen to them personally.
Todd Then it can't be that. (*To the gentleman with receding hair, who is busily rubbing hair restorer into his head*) What have you got there, my friend?
Gentleman (*happily*) Pirelli's Miracle Elixir.
Todd May I smell it?

The balding Gentleman hands Todd the bottle. Todd smells it

Pwaaugh! Chicken shit!
Gentleman What?
Todd Mixed with spittle, by the looks of it.
Gentleman Spittle and . . . ? Here, you—(*grabbing Tobias*)—what's the game? I don't want no chicken shit. I want my money back.

The onlookers laugh. The words "chicken shit" are repeated

Alfredo Pirelli enters

Alfredo Who says my miracle elixir is chicken shit?

Todd I do.

Alfredo Indeed. And who might you be, to make zees accusation?

Todd A barber. Sweeney Todd's my name. I haven't shaved the King of Naples, or performed any miracles—but I'll wager I'm a better barber than you.

Alfredo Indeed.

Todd Yes. And to prove it I accept your challenge, and as security for the wager I offer these, my razors.

Pirelli looks at the razors. Todd shows them to the onlookers

Alfredo Tobias, chairs!

Todd You accept my challenge?

Alfredo Where did you come by these?

Todd I had them off a convict long ago.

Tobias brings two high-backed chairs and sets them facing each other. Alfredo strops his razor. The onlookers make bets on the outcome

Alfredo Tobias. In the chair.

Tobias Oh, no, sir, no, not me. I mean, I've hardly got bristle, have I? Look, the merest bum fluff. It wouldn't be fair.

Alfredo In the chair!

Tobias I mean, I don't mind the shave, but I haven't got the toothache, Signor Pirelli—not even a twinge.

Alfredo (*forcing Tobias into the chair*) I will shave my assistant—and you, Signor Todd?

Todd (*motioning Anthony into the chair*) This gentleman. (*To Anthony*) I'll cause you no more pain than I can help, my friend.

Gentleman Who shall be judge?

Todd (*to the Beadle*) Why not you, sir? You have an honest face.

Beadle Well, if you insist. Are you ready, gentlemen? Begin!

Alfredo begins to shave Tobias without using any soap. Sweeney Todd rapidly lathers Anthony and begins to shave him

Alfredo Check!

The Beadle checks Tobias

Beadle A hair!

Alfredo pounces on the hair

Beadle Shave completed.

Tobias No! No!

Alfredo tips the chair with Tobias in it and begins to seek out a tooth with some devilish instrument

Todd Check!

Beadle Shave completed!

Sweeney Todd whips one of Anthony's teeth out with as little fuss as possible. After a long struggle, Alfredo also gets a tooth out, but turns to find he is too late

Beadle (*indicating Todd*) The winner!

Applause from the crowd

Alfredo I don't believe you took a tooth out! Let me see. (*He examines Anthony's mouth*) Yes. Very neat, Signor—Todd, was it? (*Giving Todd money*) Here is fifty pounds—I will bring you the rest tomorrow. Where can I find you?

Todd Fleet Street. Above Mrs Lovett's lodgings.

Alfredo Yes. You shall hear more of me, Signor. (*Going*) Tobias, come!

Alfredo exits. Tobias follows with the chairs

Beadle Remarkable! Hardly any pain at all! If you can carry out all your work as well as you've done on this gentleman, I swear you must be the most famous barber in London.

Todd I hope to become so.

Beadle (*for the benefit of the crowd*) I shall come to you in future, Mr Todd.

Todd (*after a brief pause*) You will be most welcome. (*He tips the Beadle*)

The Beadle exits

Gentleman Will you sell hair restorer?

Todd Doubtless!

The balding Gentleman wanders off

Todd starts packing away his shaving stuff

The crowd disperses, leaving Todd and Anthony

Todd I hope I didn't cause you too much pain, my friend?

Anthony None in the world. But then, I told you—it's impossible to cause me pain today. As I was walking towards . . . (*He breaks off*) But I forget myself. What of your news, my friend? Did you find your family?

Todd My wife is dead—an accident, no-one is to blame; but my daughter lives, a great man's ward.

Anthony Then there's some consolation. Will you seek to get her back?

Todd Perhaps, in time, but for the moment she is safe. I am content that she is alive and well. I shall start a new life in my old profession. This hundred pounds will make a barber of me once again.

Anthony I'm glad you're so contented.

Todd And you. You said that nothing I could do to you could cause you pain today . . .

Anthony Nothing at all. It's strange that I should travel all the world, only to find its greatest treasure here at home. No, do not laugh—though by your face I see you've guessed the cause of all my joy. As I was walking along, deep in thought, something made me stop and look up—and there above, just in the casement of her window, I saw a lady of so pure and true a countenance I could not pass the place while she stood there. The sight of her seemed to—stop my breath. I stood and gazed in such rapturous admiration that the passers-by avoided me as if I was struck mad. Just as she seemed about to leave her window, she glanced down, and her eyes met mine. What passions passed between us in that instant I cannot say, for I have never known the like before. Then modesty compelled her to avert her eyes, and she was gone; but not without a sigh that seemed to draw my soul out of my body. I enquired at once within the house who she was, and I learned she lives there with her guardian, a judge of high renown . . .

Todd A judge? What was his name?

Anthony Judge Turpin, an old and reverent man, or so the servant said. Oh, my friend, do not tell me it is the same judge of whom you spoke last night?

Todd (*lying*) No, he is dead long since. Go on, my friend, what next?

Anthony I came away to meet you here. It was just as well, for though I would have given this right arm for one hour of her company, it would not have been prudent in the state that I was in.

Todd Come, then. I have a mind to open my barber's shop in it's old place, and good Mrs Lovett has been cleaning up. I must survey her work. Will you walk with me?

Anthony If you'll not mind my talking of my love, for telling it re-fashions the event, making it happen once again, almost as sweet as when I first beheld her.

Todd Then let us go.

Todd and Anthony exit

SCENE 4

Judge Turpin's house

The Judge enters. He wears his robes and carries a scourge in one hand and an open Bible in the other

Judge (*reading*) Let him who is without guilt cast the first stone. (*He closes the book*) Can there be such a man? Is it possible that any man can live quite free of sin? Yes, I know it can be so, but I am not he. (*He takes off the robe and lays it and the Bible on a chair*) I, who by my office should be incorruptible, have ripped the blindfolds from sweet Justice's face, weighed down her scales with sin, and stained her blameless sword with innocent blood. Now, teeming flesh, take thou the recompense. An angel ravished, she who took her life for shame, a life worth thirty thousand times my own. And all for loathed lust! (*Scourging himself*) Out, out! Vile bestial man! Lascivious devil, down! (*He falls to his knees, sobbing; Johanna is heard singing offstage*) Heaven mocks my penitence, and turns my one good act to mockery.

In true contrition did I take Johanna in, made her my ward
and loved her truer than I would my own. Loved her too true, for as her
body swelled to womanhood, a cankered weed entwined itself around
that sweet flower of father feeling. That weed is lust, and now it chokes
my soul. Down, rising stench! Down! Down! (*He lashes himself into a
frenzy, moaning and shrieking. Finally he recovers himself*) We must be
what we are. I cannot change. I'll bed her lawfully—she'll be my wife.
Yes, yes. I'll give her all, and she shall tend me in my increasing age.
Draw from me this hot devil with her soft and virgin palms. Yes. Yes,
that's recompense more fitting. (*He puts on his robe*) So! Now the guilty
man is gone. The raiment of the law sits square upon my shoulders once
again, and covers o'er my shame. (*He calls*) Johanna! Daughter, come
hither to me! Johanna! Here within.

Johanna enters

Sweet daughter, why, how fair you look today. That dress becomes you.
Nay, do not turn away. It is almost a week since we have spoken close
together, and I am sorry that on that occasion I had need to reprimand
you. But it is a father's office to protect the innocent from dangers that
they can only guess at. That bold young sailor who stared so from the
street would do you harm. And you, unknowingly, encouraged him.

Johanna (*aside*) I would I had encouraged him to climb the wall that we
might stare some more. And clasp each other's hands and swear true
love.

Judge For, from your forwardness he's taken hope, and has returned
each day in hopes of seeing you.

Johanna Is that the reason that this door's been locked!

Judge It is. These things were unimportant when you were a girl, but
now you are a woman you must take more care. Smile less on those you
meet—keep from the windows. You must prepare yourself for marriage.

Johanna (*aside*) How shall I prepare myself for marriage if I may not
smile on that same gentleman?

Judge What's that, what's that?

Johanna How shall I be married? I know nobody—never leave this house.

Judge I have a husband in mind for you. Somewhat your senior in years,
it is true, but an honourable match.

Johanna Who is he?

Judge Wealthy, and much respected. Well above your station, but willing
to take you as you are. Do but marry him, and you shall want for
nothing.

Johanna (*aside*) Save love and laughter. (*To the Judge*) What is his name?

Judge He has known you since you were a child. Loved you. Watched
you—and waited, dared to hope, tended you like a father, and now—
(*he kneels*)—kneels before you.

Johanna You!

Judge Oh, I will love you, Johanna, not as a father, but as a husband
should. Be but kind to me . . .

Johanna Never!

Judge You don't know what you are saying. Let me leaf through the pages of love's book for you, and show you pleasure in a thousand guises . . . (*He clutches her around the knees and kisses her dress*)

Johanna You make yourself ridiculous, sir! Pray rise! The grave shall rather have my maidenhood than such a one as you.

The Judge scrambles to his feet

Judge The grave shall have it, then! And not some idle puppy like that sailor who has caught your eye. If you'll not marry me, then you shall never know the sweetness of a man.

Johanna So be it. For I could never know that sweetness in your bed.

The Judge makes as if to strike her. Johanna stands her ground, and he regains his composure with difficulty

Judge You are too rash. Ponder on what I've said. I must away to court. On my return we will speak further.

The Judge exits

Johanna The ways of Providence are strange, for in the darkest hour there is a gleam of hope. In his agitation he has left the door unlocked. I may again gaze from the window in the hope that my love will come. (*She goes to the window*) Oh, come on wings of love so swift and bear me hence at once. But till that time I'll sing to pass the hours.

SCENE 5

The barber shop

Todd and Mrs Lovett are working

Todd So, we are ready at last!

Mrs Lovett What d'you mean, "at last"? There's no-one else could have cleaned this place up in the time I have. And you haven't been no help, neither, fidgeting with that thing all the while.

Todd (*holding up the razor*) My friend here is impatient, Mrs Lovett.

Mrs Lovett I dare say he is, but put him away for the minute. He's making me nervous.

Todd closes the razor and puts it down

'Scuse me asking, but are you sure you're going to go through with this? I mean, you was always so sensitive, weren't you? Remember how you fainted away that time when you cut yourself bad.

Todd That was not Sweeney Todd who fainted, Mrs Lovett.

Mrs Lovett Oh, I know, I know. It was the other fellow who looked like you. You don't have to pretend to me, you know. Aren't you a little bit nervous?

Todd A nervous barber won't be long in business. But—yes, yes, I have my doubts. The event must witness whether I can master them.

Mrs Lovett (*looking out of the window*) Well, here comes the event now. Nice-looking fellow an' all. I'll be off.

Mrs Lovett exits

Todd (*taking up the razor*) Keep steadfast to the purpose. Remember your revenge.

Footsteps are heard. Anthony enters

Oh, it is you.

Anthony I understand your disappointment. I'm no company for anyone these days. Seven days I've watched and waited at her window, but not once has she appeared. The Judge refuses to admit me to the house. What would you do in my place?

Footsteps are heard approaching

Todd Faint heart never won fair lady. In your place I should not leave her window till I'd seen her—were it a week, a month, a year even.

Pirelli and Tobias enter

Good day, gentlemen.

Anthony Perhaps I misinterpreted it all. Perhaps she glanced at me in curiosity and was offended by my stare. What do you think?

Todd No, no, it cannot be. So to her once again.

Anthony Without much hope, then, I will go.

Anthony exits

Todd Now, sir. (*He indicates a chair*)

Alfredo (*sitting*) A matter of business. Thank you, Signor.

Todd I hope you bear me no ill will over our little wager.

Alfredo No ill will in the world, Mr Todd. I have come to settle my debt. (*Indicating Tobias*) But there is another little business . . .

Todd (*to Tobias*) You look half starved, lad. Would you not care for a pie? To tell you the truth, you are my first customers—perhaps you'll bring me luck. Go down these back stairs to Mrs Lovett's shop and say I sent you. She'll give you food and drink.

Tobias That I will.

Tobias exits

Alfredo Now, Mr—Todd, as I have said, I bear you no grudge at all as a result of our little wager—in fact, I positively thank you for it. It has long been in my mind to retire from barbering—I find the life rather strenuous—and our little competition has given me an idea as to how I might earn a living without overtiring myself.

Todd Indeed. How?

Alfredo You are a better barber than I could ever hope to be . . .

Todd You are too kind.

Alfredo So I say to myself, why should you not work for both of us? For you are so good a barber that I would almost say that I have never seen the like—except once, when I was a boy, I was taken to have a troublesome tooth removed—yes? And the barber-surgeon who removed it was as good, I think, as you—yes? Not better, no. But just as good. In fact, so good that I could almost swear that it was the same man. But that cannot be, can it? For I have since found out that that barber was transported many years ago.

Todd There must be some mistake.

Alfredo Of course, you cannot be the same, but it is odd, is it not, that you should both possess a very unusual set of razors. Is not that one of them in your hand now?

Todd I told you, I had them off a convict, many years ago . . .

Alfredo (*sharply, in a cockney accent*) All right, you can leave the cackle, Mr—Todd, or whatever fancy name you've given yourself. My name's Alf Spiral, and I know who you really are. The Beadle might like to know an' all, mightn't he? So you'd best just pipe down an' listen to me. Now, I'm prepared to be generous—we'll go halves on any money you make in this shop of yours. I can't say fairer than that, can I? And in return I let you keep your little secret. Okay?

Todd You slimy, crimping son of a . . .

Alfredo Now don't go calling me names, it's all in a matter of business. I mean, I don't want to go to the Beadle—not unless you twist me arm, like. So what do you say? (*Offering his hand*) Is it a bargain?

Todd Needs must when the devil drives. (*He shakes hands with him*)

Alfredo You are a one, ain't you? Right, then! I'll be round the first Tuesday of every month to get me share—that suit you?

Todd nods agreement, then goes to the window

Good! And don't try no tricks, mind, or you know what'll happen.

Todd You're a fine one to talk of tricks! A man who breaks his word the moment he's given it.

Alfredo What d'you mean?

Todd Here comes the Beadle now, and the officers are with him.

Alfredo goes to the window

Alfredo I never sent for 'em. Where?

Todd (*making room for him*) There! Coming this way.

Alfredo I can't see . . .

Todd grabs him by the throat

Aaaagh!

Todd strangles him

Todd So! Not as I would wish—my razor's dry. Still, the end's the same.

Tobias (*off*) Master? Are you there?

Todd The boy! Curse him!

Tobias You've got an appointment with the tailor in an hour. You told me to remind you.

Todd Hide him, hide him! (*He opens a chest and pushes Alfredo's body inside. As he drops the lid, one of the hands remains trapped outside*)

Tobias enters

Tobias You did say specially to remind you, master—oh, he's not here.

Todd No, he was called away.

Tobias Oh well, I don't suppose he'll be long.

Todd (*aside*) Longer than you think, my friend.

Tobias (*going to sit on the chest*) I'd better wait for him.

Todd turns and sees the hand

Todd The hand!

Tobias I wouldn't mind if he never came back. No such luck! He'd come out of his grave to make sure I wasn't skiving, that bloke would.

The fingers of the hand move and tug at Tobias's coat. He pushes it away

You know, it was marvellous the way you whipped that gentleman's tooth out. Hardly hurt him at all. (*Rubbing his jaw ruefully*) Wish I could say the same for my guvnor; but then, he's not an artist like you—well, stands to reason, you've only got to look at his hands—like great lumps of meat, they are.

The hand tug at Tobias's coat again. He absently pushes it away

Todd Why don't you have another pie downstairs, while you wait for him?

Tobias Ah, now you're talking, sir.

As Tobias starts to get up the hand holds on to his coat-tail, preventing him from moving away

'Ere, I must have got caught on a nail . . .

Todd (*aside*) Aye, a fingernail! (*He goes and pulls the hand away*) Don't distress yourself—there! Now you are freed.

Tobias Thanks, sir. Well now, I will take you up on that offer of another pie, if you don't mind. Just till the guvnor gets back, though as far as I'm concerned, he can go to the devil.

Tobias exits

Todd (*fetching his razor and going to the chest*) That he can! And quickly,

too! (*He opens the chest and cuts Alfredo's throat*) So! I have seen death
a thousand times—what man has been transported and has not? But
then the body bore a multitude of hardships, and still breath flickered
on. Yet now—behold! I turn my wrist, and my life pumps forth its
ruddy stream, and then is quenched all in an instant. And where, before,
who knows what hopes and loves resided, now sits oblivion with his
stony stare.

SCENE 6

The Judge's house

Johanna is standing by the window. The clock chimes

Johanna He will not come. The Judge was right, he did but trifle with me.
Why then did he return each day to look for me? That sure is proof!
And yet it's also proof that love's a fickle flower to blossom but a week
and then be gone. For if my sight may kindle in his breast, why, so the
sight of others may, and opportunity, the wind of chance, fan theirs to
blaze and blow my tender flame quite out. It's for the best. For perfect
love is love on both sides equal matched. Had I been in the street and
he above, I would have made my bed upon the stones. Nor ate nor slept
—not for a week, but for an age till I might once again behold my love.
(*Pause*) He will not come! Oh wretched girl! Condemned to marry
where I hate. Marry a man I fear has wronged me much already. For
when at prayer he sometimes cries upon my mother in accents terrible,
but then the words are jumbled so the sense of them is all but lost. And
yet I fear the worst.

There is the sound of a stone hitting the window

What noise is that? (*She looks out*) 'Tis he! He comes! Away with
maiden fears. Hence modesty—inhabit other cheeks. I'll let him in.
(*She opens the door*)

Anthony enters

Anthony Forgive my boldness. Believe me when I say I'd rather suffer
hell and all its torments than harm your honour. But how else may I
speak to you when all the doors are shut against me? (*Staring at her*)
Oh, fair Johanna!

Johanna Sir, you are ahead of me. Your face is stamped indelible upon
the picture of my mind, but what name shall there attend it?

Anthony Anthony Hope. Captain of the good ship *Bountiful*. (*He looks
around, worried*) I am afraid my presence here will taint your name.

Johanna Oh, sir, my honour was in pawn to you the moment that I saw
you. I am yours to deal with as you will. For though it ill becomes a
maid to speak thus, I did love you even as I did look upon you.

Anthony Oh, happy man! Like love for love I offer. Haste the day when the church bells make us one.

Johanna And there you make me sad. The Judge will rather see me dead than married to another. This very morning he has sworn that if I will not consent to share his bed, then I shall never marry.

Anthony An old man such as he? (*Thoughtfully*) It ill becomes a child to thwart its parents, and to do so in important matters courts disaster. But in such a case as this—the parent so unnatural, his wishes counter to the child's most absolute desire, we surely may o'erleap that step. My love, I now make trial of your words so sweetly uttered. Will you attempt a deed that makes us one? Will you elope with me this very night?

Johanna This very hour.

Anthony I must have time to organize a coach, some horses, and a place where you may stay in honour till our marriage. Give me until tonight.

Johanna Until tonight? I fear some mishap. He may return and lock this door again—it was by chance he left it free today. But if it must be " 'Till tonight", then I will leave my bedroom casement open that you may scale the garden walls and bear me from this place. And so you do not miss your way, I'll leave a candle burning at the window till the dawn approaches.

Anthony Do so, and do not fear, for I will come as surely as that dawn. I must about the business.

Johanna Go not so soon. What, will you leave me so?

Anthony I go to make us one.

Johanna Then take this ring in token of my love. It was my mother's, and is most precious to me—but now I take it off to give it thee.

Anthony (*taking the ring*) I'll guard it with my life. Now sweet, adieu.

Johanna Nay—stay a moment! Let's seal our compact with a tender kiss.

Anthony does not move

Why do you hesitate?

Anthony Oh, not for lack of love, but rather what may follow. My passion's past the curb of honour. I fear that, all unbridled, it may run if I should tease it with a single kiss.

Johanna Then tease it now for me.

They kiss. Anthony breaks away

Anthony Lest I forget myself. Adieu, until tonight.

Anthony exits

Johanna Until tonight. Tonight. Tonight!

SCENE 7

The Courtroom

The Judge is on the bench, sentencing an unseen prisoner. The Beadle stands close by

Judge It well becomes the sacred office that I hold to temper justice with a show of mercy—but in this case I cannot. The vilest of voluptuaries, a ravisher, a cutpurse, and a pimp: only one sentence can serve your turn. (*To the Beadle*) The cap! (*He takes the cap from the Beadle and puts it on*) You are sentenced to be hanged by the neck until you are dead, and may the Lord have mercy on your soul. Away with him! The Court will adjourn. (*He removes the cap and descends from the bench*)

Beadle Thank you, your Honour. Just the sentence we wanted.

Judge Was he guilty?

Beadle Well, if he didn't do that one, he's surely done enough we don't know of to warrant hanging.

Judge (*aside*) What man has not?

Beadle Your Honour! Er—your Honour, I hope you'll excuse me saying so, but—you don't look at all well. I mean your eyes are all bloodshot, and you—well, you always look so neat in court, but you haven't even shaved this morning.

Judge No—no, I was distracted. She must consent to marry me—she must. I'll speak with her as soon as I return.

Beadle Speak with who, your Honour?

Judge What? Oh, my ward—Johanna.

Beadle Ah! Well, your Honour, if it's her you're going to speak with— you'll want to look your best, won't you?

Judge My best—yes.

Beadle I know just the man to freshen you up with the closest shave you ever had. Amazing barber, he is. Never seen the like! Pulled a tooth in the market-place the other day, and the gent hardly flinched.

Judge Yes, he will serve. Where is his shop?

Beadle Hardly a minute from here. I'll walk with you . . .

Judge No, I'll walk alone. I must think. Yes. Where . . .

Beadle Fleet Street, his shop is. His name's Sweeney Todd.

Judge Todd. Yes. (*Going*) She must consent. She must.

Beadle Farewell, your Honour.

SCENE 8

The Barber shop

Todd is cleaning his razor. Mrs Lovett enters

Mrs Lovett That lad Tobias Ragg's eating me out of house and home.

He must have hollow legs. How long before that Eyetalian gets back?
(*She sits on the chest*)

Todd Not till judgement day.

Mrs Lovett You mean you've done for him? Well! Who'd have thought
it? Where is he?

Todd points to the chest. She jumps up

What! He ain't! Can I have a look?

Todd nods agreement. She opens the chest

Oooh! You did do for him, didn't you? But why? He didn't do you
no harm. I mean, he weren't to do with—what happened before.

Todd He recognized me. Tried to blackmail me.

Mrs Lovett Did he now? Well, he won't be doin' no more of that, will
he? Enough to make you come all over gooseflesh, see him lying there
like that.

Todd Then shut the lid. (*He goes to do so*)

Mrs Lovett Just a minute! You said I could have a look! Fancy him
coming up here all unsuspecting like, and then . . . (*She makes an
expressive noise*) And his lad, sitting down there all the while, not
knowing—hey, what about that lad? Does he suspect?

Todd No, he's a simple fool. (*He picks up his razor*) But you'd best send
him up—for safety.

Mrs Lovett Oh, do you have to? I've taken quite a fancy to the lad. I
always like a good healthy appetite on a man . . .

Todd (*looking out of the window*) The boy can wait if that man steps this
way. Impossible! He's coming here! Oh, Providence is kind.

Mrs Lovell What are you rattling on about?

Todd Judge Turpin!

Mrs Lovett Coming here? I'd better clear off.

Todd Aye, quickly. And keep that brat downstairs.

Mrs Lovett goes quickly down the back stairs

Footsteps are heard approaching. Todd waits calmly

The Judge enters

Judge Mr Todd?

Todd At your service—your Honour.

Judge A shave! (*He hands his stick and hat to Todd*)

Todd (*putting them down*) With pleasure, sir. (*He helps the Judge off with
his coat*) May I enquire what happy chance directed you to my poor
shop? (*He hangs up the coat*)

Judge (*sitting*) The Beadle recommended you.

Todd Let's hope he follows after.

Judge What's that?

Todd (*going to his table*) I must work up a lather. (*He starts to lather the Judge's face*) Is it possible that we have met before, your Honour?

Judge Hm! Your face does look familiar. But then, I see so many. Were you ever on a jury?

Todd I went to court once—long ago. But not upon a jury.

Judge A witness, then?

Todd (*aside*) A witness to your infamy, that's true.

Judge What was the case? Perhaps I can recall it.

Todd A trifling matter. I doubt that you'll remember. (*Aside*) Oh, but you shall, you shall. (*Aloud*) Now that I think of it, it was you who tried the case. I hope that I don't bore you, sir?

Judge No, I—my mind's elsewhere. I have a headache.

Todd Why did you not say so before, your Honour? A damp cloth upon the eyes is very soothing for a headache. May I? (*He puts a cloth over the Judge's eyes*)

Judge Thank you. You are most kind, master barber. I'll not forget it.

Todd (*aside*) No, you shall not. Not one jot! See how he sits there, blind, helpless like some new-dropped kitten—warm and full of trust. Was my wife's throat as bare as that when he with musty kisses forced on her his foul attentions? To the purpose. (*He shaves the Judge*) This case I told you of, concerned my wife—though not directly.

Judge Ah, there's many a man . . .

Todd Hold still, your Honour, that I may shave your lip. (*Aside*) One slice, and he would kiss no more. (*He shaves*) Now! (*Aloud*) You may recall my wife. Her name was . . .

Anthony bursts into the room

Anthony My friend!

Todd Ha! (*He breaks away from the chair*)

Anthony Oh, you were right! Johanna is mine! My patience has been rewarded. She will elope with me this very night.

Todd What!

Anthony Johanna, Judge Turpin's daughter—she is mine!

Judge (*tearing the towel from his face and leaping up*) Yours! Not while I breathe!

Todd Lost! Lost!

Anthony Judge Turpin!

Judge The same! And this I swear, never more shall you behold Johanna, for I will put her where no man can enter—unless it be to lose his wits. To Bedlam shall she straight, and Jonas Fogg's asylum.

A dumb show is enacted, showing Johanna being taken within the asylum gates

Anthony No, no! You cannot! She is not mad!

Judge Well, if she be not mad to love a man like you, she will be before a year is out. Old Jonas keeps 'em close. (*He goes towards the door*)

Anthony No, no!

Judge Away!
Todd Your shave, your Honour . . .
Judge No, master barber, I'll not stay here. I don't like your friends.

The Judge exits

Anthony Oh, I will drown myself for sorrow! (*Rushing out*) No! You must relent!

Anthony exits

Todd Escaped! Curse Judge! Curse sailor—curse myself! When comes a second chance? My poor Johanna!

Mrs Lovett enters

Mrs Lovett Here, what's up? Judge Turpin's just run through my shop like the devil himself was after him.
Todd He was, but ran too slow.
Mrs Lovett And no sooner had I got me breath back when the other gentleman came roaring through, tearing his hair and sobbing fit to burst hisself.
Todd Poor Anthony.
Mrs Lovett You haven't beer found out already?
Todd No, no, nothing like that.
Mrs Lovett Well, that's a mercy.
Todd A second chance may come. It must, it shall! Until it does, I'll pass the time in practice on less honoured throats.
Mrs Lovett I don't understand you. You let that Judge escape one minute, and the next you're on about slicing up any Tom, Dick or Harry. This revenge business don't half blow hot and cold, it don't.
Todd Revenge? Oh, no! The work's its own reward. For now I find I have a taste for blood, and all the world's my meat.
Mrs Lovett There you go again. You've got to start being practical, believe me, or you'll come to a sticky end. I mean, what about this Eyetalian in here? What are you going to do with him? And what about his lad downstairs? Such a cheery soul, he is. If trade was better I'd take him on to help me, but . . .
Todd (*going to the chest*) You're right! First we'll dispose of him, then think about the boy. (*He opens the chest and looks down at the body*)
Mrs Lovett That's what I like to hear. Bit of common sense. What'll you do with him?
Todd Bury his body in some secret place where no-one will ever find it.
Mrs Lovett Do we have to? Seems a shame to bury him.

Todd looks at her.

With business so bad.
Todd I don't understand. He'll eat no more pies . . .

Mrs Lovett No, he couldn ι *eat* them—but he might help in the *making* of 'em—in a manner of speaking.

Todd The boy—Tobias Ragg, you mean?

Mrs Lovett Well, he might help sell them, perhaps—but that gent in there—it would be a pity to waste him. I mean, he is nice and plump, isn't he?

Todd begins to understand

And with meat the price it is these days . . .

Todd Oh sweet, delectable, rare and choice. By my assistance you shall never want for meat, Mrs Lovett. Your pies shall be the wonder of the town. For every customer who comes up here shall serve the ones below.

They both start to giggle, then fall into each other's arms laughing helplessly, as—

the CURTAIN *falls*

ACT II

Fleet Street. Day

Outside the pie shop Tobias Ragg is drumming trade. A crowd gathers, among them the Beggar Woman

Tobias Ladies and gentlemen, when God first made the world he made it good, and put upon it for our pleasure sweet sounds and sights to glad our ears and eyes and gratify our senses, but he neglected us in one respect. He gave us tongues and gullets, stomachs too, but nothing extraordinary to feed them with. Oh yes, he gave us bread and meat and water- -but nothing so rare as that which thrills our eye. But what he's left undone, good Mrs Lovett's rectified with her most succulent pies. You know their reputation, and well do they deserve it. For there is about them a flavour never surpassed or even equalled; the pastry— oh, gentlemen, the pastry is of the most delicate construction, lovingly crimped at its edges with her own fair hand—its top baked to a rich and golden brown, and its underneath impregnated with the aroma of a delicious gravy that defies description. Do but lift that heavenly canopy and there below lie juicy chunks of meat so tender, so exquisitely inviting that you will not, cannot, put it back. Oh, gentlemen, the fat and lean are so artistically mixed up, the lean so soft that you may tease the tendrils of its flesh apart merely by revolving the tip of your tongue. (*He demonstrates*) Oh . . . (*He appears overcome*) Oh, gentlemen, I speak from experience. I know, for I have teased those tendrils. Oh, ladies— gentlemen, can you deny yourselves such bliss? Oh, I cannot. (*He eats*) You'd best hurry, before they're all sold out.

Some of the crowd enter the pie shop—others disperse

The Beggar Woman touches Tobias on the arm

I'm sorry, duck, I've got no money.

Beggar Woman I don't want money. (*Pause*) What's his name? That barber—him up there?

Tobias Him? Oh, his name's Sweeney Todd. Him and Mrs Lovett go half shares in the pie shop, and the trade we're doing at the moment, that's a tidy bit, believe me.

Beggar Woman Where is he from?

Tobias I dunno. The first I saw of him he scotched my old guvnor, Alf Spiral, in St Dunstan's market-place. Now, I wonder what happened to him? Funny, the way he disappeared.

Beggar Woman Disappeared?

Tobias Yes. We come round on a matter of business to see Mr Todd, and while I was eating a pie downstairs, he went off, and I never saw him again. Not that I'm complaining, mind. Stroke of luck, that was, 'cos Mrs Lovett offered me the job that same day—said if Alf came she'd buy me off of him. Thank Gawd, he hasn't, so far. (*Sniffing*) Cor, there ain't half an 'orrible smell round 'ere. Shockin', it is!

Beggar Woman It comes from the cellars round about.

Tobias They ought to do something about it.

Beggar Woman Have you been down to your mistress's cellars?

Tobias No such luck. That's where she bakes her pies—I wouldn't mind half an hour down there doing a bit of damage, I can tell you. Look, I'm off now. I got work to do. But here's a halfpenny—it's all I got, cross me heart.

Beggar Woman God bless you, lad.

Tobias (*about to go*) And you, mum.

Beggar Woman Wait. Don't eat those pies no more. Don't eat 'em!

Tobias You might as well tell me not to go to sleep. Why not, for the love of Gawd?

Beggar Woman I—I'm not sure. But I fear the contents are not savoury.

Tobias Oh-ho. You've not tasted 'em, or you wouldn't say that.

Tobias exits

The Beggar Woman stands for a moment, deep in thought

The Gentleman with the receding hair who was in the market-place enters furtively

Gentleman Excuse me, can you direct me to Mr Sweeney Todd's establishment?

Beggar Woman What do you want there?

Gentleman That's none of your business. Ah, I see it there.

Beggar Woman Don't go in—oh, go elsewhere.

Gentleman I've tried everywhere else. This is my last hope.

The Gentleman enters the shop

The Beggar Woman stands watching for a moment, then starts to go

Beggar Woman Alms! Alms for a poor unfortunate woman . . .

The Beggar Woman exits

SCENE 2

The Barber Shop

The chair is now in position. Sweeney Todd is pacing about, a trifle bored

Todd Trade flourishes, my razor sleeps to wake again and glut himself when custom comes. A pretty toy, this chair—I never tire of it. (*He demonstrates the chair*) Yet I must hold myself in check. Lately I've been impatient, and have been tempted to dispose of men with wives and families, men whose absence would be missed. That's folly! Orphans and strangers to the town, men without ties or friends—those are the customers I like to see. Ah! I grow bored. (*He comes down to the audience*) Does no-one want a shave?

Gentleman (*off*) Mr Todd?

Todd In happy time . . .

The balding Gentleman enters

Come in, sir. Shave?

Gentleman No. I've come about—well, it's a bit ticklish, you understand. (*He takes off his hat*) Do you remember me?

Todd Well, you face is familiar . . .

Gentleman I was at St Dunstan's market-place, the day you won that wager.

Todd Now it comes back to me. You were the man who bought the chick . . .

Gentleman Pirelli's Miracle Elixir, yes, that's me. And notwithstanding what it was, I rubbed it in. But it didn't do no good, of course, as you can see. It's got worse.

Todd Well, surely that's not so bad, there are many men with bald heads in the world. Some say it is a sign of potency.

Gentleman Well, my wife didn't.

Todd Then buy a wig.

Gentleman Oh, that's all very well for most people, but it don't help me at all. You see, Mr Todd, my head's just the bit that shows . . . Mr Todd, can I rely on you? If what I'm going to tell you ever got out in the profession I'd be ruined—not that that makes any odds, I'm ruined already; I'm thinking of emigrating, it's got so bad.

Todd (*aside*) The fellow grows interesting. (*Aloud*) You can rely on my discretion. (*He seats the Gentleman in the chair*)

Gentleman Well—(*he unbuttons his shirt to expose his chest*)—look at that. Nothing!

Todd But yet I do not see the problem. Many men are short of hair on the body—I have very little myself.

Gentleman Oh, Mr Todd, you should have seen me when I was in me prime. Oh, then my chest was like a field of waving corn, and not this blighted stubble. Mr Todd, I swear to you, six months ago there wasn't a hairier man in all England. Legs, arms, back, you never saw such a tangle. And it made me fortune for me, me hair.

Todd works the mechanism of the chair, but the Gentleman stands up and moves away. Todd returns the chair to its original position just as the Gentleman turns back

I'm a prize-fighter, you see; not championship class or nothing like that, but I made a good living on account of me hair. "The Human Bear" they billed me as, and I used to fight very dirty, foul a lot like. Then, six months ago, I had a disappoinment in love, as you might say. Me missus went off with Tom Stokes the Fighting Blacksmith. He's real class—you might have heard of him—and she took the kiddies with her and left me all on me lonesome.

Todd (*aside*) Better and better. (*Aloud*) Pray sit, sir. I'll examine you.

The Gentleman sits. Todd goes to prepare to work the chair

Gentleman And ever since then it's been coming out in handfuls. And I can't get work no more—I mean, look at me, I'm as smooth as a baby's bum.

Todd Your troubles are at an end, my friend.

Todd is about to do for the Gentleman, but the Gentleman rises and clasps him by the hands

Gentleman Oh, Mr Todd, you mean that you can help me?

Todd (*aside*) Aye, restless fool. (*Aloud*) Do but sit, sir.

Gentleman (*still standing*) Oh, if you can—I mean, I've tried everything. I even had a sort of wig made, for the whole body. I don't know where they got the hair from—Newgate or some such, I shouldn't wonder 'cos it was—well—it had some little visitors in it. But it weren't no good anyway, one of the legs started coming adrift in the second round and I had to lie down and be counted out, and I wasn't s'posed to do that till the eighth. They booed me, Mr Todd. Booed me.

Todd (*consoling him as he leads him back to the chair*) I'll see what I can do.

Gentleman It's making a laughing-stock of me, Mr Todd. You won't tell anyone, will you?

Todd (*putting him in the chair*) Your secret's safe with me. (*Aside*) And mine will be with you, for dead men tell no tales. (*Aloud*) Sit still now, and I'll end your worries. (*He takes a pointed instrument from his box of instruments and hides it behind his back*) Now let me see your chest. (*He examines the Gentleman's chest*)

Gentleman Oh, if you can, I'll be for ever grateful.

Sweeney Todd plunges the instrument into the Gentleman's chest

Aaaaagh!

Todd (*stifling the Gentleman's scream*) That does not sound like gratitude, my friend. But now you will sit still. (*He works the mechanism*)

The Gentleman disappears

So, hairless fool, farewell! But now—yes, Johanna! This ape has given me a scheme to rescue her. Yes. I'll ponder on it. (*Calling*) Mrs Lovett! Are you there? Attend to the cellar, if you will.

Mrs Lovett (*off*) Right you are! I'll just finish rolling out me pastry and be down there.

SCENE 3

Outside Jonas Fogg's Asylum

A bell tolls dismally. Anthony Hope enters and stares upwards

Anthony Is there no justice in the world, nor none in Heaven, that all my prayers remain unanswered? How can a just and Christian God sit over us and watch a world where evil flourishes unchecked whilst virtue ends in madness? Oh, my sweet Johanna, these stones shall be my pillow and the cheerless rain my only succour till again we are together. But that may not be until the grave, alas.

From a distance we hear Johanna's song—very sad now

Her voice! Why then, she lives—and so may I again. (*He calls quietly*) Johanna! Johanna!

The singing stops

What made her stop so suddenly? Has someone done her harm? (*Shouting*) Johanna! I will tear down these walls or leave these hands as bleeding stumps when I can do no more. Johanna! Johanna!

The Beadle enters

Beadle Now then, young man, I've had complaints of you, Mr Fogg says as how you're disturbing his patients with all this racket. Now move along, unless you want to join that lot inside.

Anthony There is a woman has been placed in there unlawfully.

Beadle Are you making a formal complaint?

Anthony I am.

Beadle Complaints, complaints, complaints. Everyone's always complaining. If it's not the lewd woman in Drury Lane it's the foul smell in Fleet Street, and if it's not that it's some tale of woe from the likes of you. What's her name, then?

Anthony Johanna.

Beadle That wouldn't be Judge Turpin's ward, now, would it?

Anthony He is not fit to claim that title—but yes, 'tis she.

Beadle Now you watch your step, young man. That's slander, that is. Can't have the likes of you shouting your mouth off about your elders and betters, can we? And as for his ward, she's mad all right—I put her in there myself. So—(*he clears his throat and continues very formally*)— having investigated your complaint I find that there is no truth in it whatsoever, and that it is a dangerous and wicked fabrication. (*He drops the formality*) Look, son, take a bit of friendly advice, forget about this here Johanna. She's not for you. Anyway, there's plenty of other fish in the sea—you should know that.

Anthony I will not rest till she be free.

Beadle All right, if that's the way you want it. I give yer fair warning, if I catch you babbling this pack of lies around the town I'll run you in. Go on, be off with you, and you can tell your barber friend Todd I've

had orders to investigate his place as soon as I can spare the time.
There's a smell coming from around there fair makes you want to vomit.
You tell him I'll be round, And no more of this complaining nonsense,
mind.

Anthony (*aside*) Authority's overturned. The age is sick, and desperate
remedies alone will serve.

Anthony exits

Beadle I dunno what's the matter with youngsters today—always bloody
complaining, they are.

SCENE 4

Mrs Lovett's Pie Shop

Mrs Lovett is chopping at her table. Todd is sitting close by

Todd Must you do that now?

Mrs Lovett There's only twenty-four hours in a day, you know, and there's
so much to do . . .

Todd I have a headache.

Mrs Lovett Have you, dear? Oh, I am sorry. I'll be done in a jiffy. (*Chopping vigorously*) But waste not, want not! And these black puddings are
selling very well, you know. There, that'll do it. (*She pushes the pieces of
meat and fat into the mixing-bowl and starts to stir the black pudding mix*)
I'm fair worn out with all this work. Fair worn out. Not that I'm complaining, mind, what with the trade we're doing and the overheads so
low, like. You know, Mr Todd, we'll be able to pack it in and retire
soon. You know, I've always fancied living by the seaside. Open a
little guest house, or something. I mean, you could do the odd visitor,
just to keep your hand in, like, or you could open a little barber's shop
on the front if that weren't enough. Now where have I put them seasonings? (*She finds the seasonings*) Here we are. (*She shakes out a salt and
pepper mixture*) My old mother used to say you could make scrag-end
taste like chicken if you was particular with your seasoning. Now, what
was I saying? Oh, yes, wouldn't it be beautiful by the sea, all that fresh
air—and you're partial to a piece of fish for your tea, aren't you?
Or a shrimp or two, all done in butter? I say, you like a bit of fish, don't
you, Mr Todd? (*She approaches Sweeney Todd*) Well, how about it?
We can't go on like this, you know.

Todd Like what?

Mrs Lovett You living above, like, and us not married. People are beginning to talk.

Todd Let them.

Mrs Lovett Typical! Men! Oh, it's all very well for you, but it's not so
nice for a woman, I can tell you. All sorts of names they're calling me

behind my back, I shouldn't wonder. Well, it's not nice, is it? (*Still holding the bowl, she sits on Todd's knee*) I mean, you do love me just a teensy bit, don't yer? (*She nibbles at his ear coquettishly*)

Todd Indeed I do. (*He kisses her*)

Mrs Lovett Ooooh—(*putting the bowl on the table*)—here me hands are all mucky. Just let me give 'em a wipe. (*She wipes her hands on her apron*) Now then. (*She cuddles him with relish*) How about a little guest house, then? I'd keep it nice as pie, I would. Warm yer slippers by the fire, fetch you a jug when you wanted one, polish yer razors up regular. You wouldn't want for nothing with me looking after you.

Todd (*kissing her between every word*) The Judge—the Beadle—first . . .

Mrs Lovett (*getting up and indignantly smoothing her skirt*) I thought you'd packed that revenge caper in. Still moaning after your Lucy, are you? Still wishing she hadn't of poisoned herself?

Todd There, there. Now, Sweeney Todd has never had a wife—has he?

Mrs Lovett No, but that other fellow did.

Todd But you don't love that other fellow, do you? You love Sweeney Todd. Come, come.

Mrs Lovett sits on his knee again

Mrs Lovett I suppose so, but . . .

Sweeney Todd kisses her again

Ooooh! I could eat you up I could. Yer so lovely.

Tobias Ragg enters

Tobias (*on his way out again*) Oooops. Sorry to intrude.

Todd No, stay, Tobias. What is it you want?

Tobias Well, Mr Todd, I was wondering if there was any odd pies like —er—going to waste, like . . .

Mrs Lovett There's one over there you can have.

Tobias goes to get the pie

(*To Todd*) It's a bargain, then. You do the Judge and Beadle first, and then we'll look for premises by the sea.

Todd Agreed.

Tobias Can I have a drop of ale, Mrs Lovett?

Mrs Lovett 'Course you can.

Tobias goes to pour himself some ale

(*To Todd*) Aren't you going to propose, then?

Todd (*aside*) The woman grows ridiculous, but I must humour her. (*Aloud*) When Judge and Beadle are both dead, my dear.

Mrs Lovett Oh well. I've waited so long, I suppose it can't do no harm to wait a bit longer.

Tobias comes to them, eating his pie

Tobias (*with his mouth full*) De-licious, Mrs L., de-licious.

Mrs Lovett Oh, he's a boy, i'n't he—loves my cooking, he does.

Tobias I don't know how you do it, Mrs L, I really don't. That old woman wants her head examined.

Mrs Lovett What old woman?

Tobias That old beggar woman what hangs around sometimes. Said she didn't think these pies of yours was very savoury. I told her straight she couldn't never have tasted one or she wouldn't say that.

Todd What passed between you?

Tobias Oh, she's just a silly old nit bag. She asked some questions about you and then said as how Mrs L's pies wasn't tasty. She's a bit daft, if you ask me.

Todd (*aside to Mrs Lovett*) Who is this woman?

Mrs Lovett (*aside to Todd*) I know no more than you, but she grows dangerous.

Todd (*aside to Mrs Lovett*) So does the boy.

Mrs Lovett (*aside to Todd*) Dispose of them.

Todd (*aside to Mrs Lovett*) Yes, but later. The boy is still of use. (*Aloud*) Tobias, you have done your work so well that, if such were possible, Mrs Lovett now has too much custom. She cannot bake her pies as fast as they are eaten . . .

Tobias Oh, Mr Todd, you're not going to turn me out, are you?

Todd No, no, nothing like that, Tobias, that would be gross ingratitude. (*Aside*) And folly, too. (*Aloud*) We thought that since you liked her pies so much you might assist her in the cooking of them. Why, you could eat your fill of pies, and they'd be piping hot—straight from the oven.

Tobias Oh, Mr Todd—could I?

Todd Of course, of course. (*To Mrs Lovett*) My dear, why don't you take him to the cellar now—so he can start at once? (*Aside to her*) Then lock him in, he'll never see another soul to tell of what he knows.

Mrs Lovett (*aside*) That will serve. (*Aloud*) Yes. Come, Tobias. I'll explain your duties.

Tobias and Mrs Lovett exit

Todd The boy goes willingly. Why shouldn't he? He'll make the pies and eat them and be happy. Many a man would envy his position—withdrawn from the struggles and toils of bare existence, amply provided with his board and lodgings—'twould be astonishing if he were otherwise than satisfied.

Anthony enters

Good morrow, Anthony.

Anthony Is it good morrow?

Todd Still so sad?

Anthony helps himself to ale and puts a coin on the counter

Anthony And ever shall be, till Johanna's free. Yet that seems further off than ever. Today, as I was standing outside her grim prison, the Beadle chanced along. It seems the keeper of that place complains of me, and I must now deny myself all hopes of hearing my poor lady's voice. For that same Beadle was the one first thrust her in there by the Judge's orders, and now he forbids me to go near the place.

Todd 'Tis harsh.

Anthony And by the way, he said he'd shortly call on you, to investigate the foul smell hereabouts.

Todd (*aside*) The Beadle coming here—that's good, that's good. (*Aloud*) Well, Anthony, put on a brighter face, for I've devised a scheme to set Johanna free.

Anthony To set her free? Tell me, what is it? (*He sits*)

Todd A customer mentioned today that he had sometime purchased hair from Newgate Prison, seeking to make a wig from it. And if from there, why not from Jonas Fogg? That gains me entrance, for I'll masquerade as one who makes such wigs, and once inside . . .

Anthony No, let me go! I could not bear to idly wait while you attempted this. Let me disguise myself and take the chance, for I will set her free or die in the attempt.

Todd It shall be so, but send a letter first to state your business and say that your particular need is for some hair of that same colour as Johanna's. Describe the shade exactly, that he may show her to you— and then effect escape.

Anthony I will. And this will serve our turn. (*He draws a pistol*) I'll purchase a disguise and draft the letter straight, that you may check it through to see there's nothing in it wrongly writ, for I know nought of wigs. Oh, my dear friend, I owe you my life, for I'd resolved to blow my brains out, and with this very instrument.

Todd 'Tis life for life. You saved me from the sea.

Anthony I must about it. So, farewell.

Anthony exits

Todd Farewell! Farewell, Johanna. My dear daughter whom I have not seen these many years. Whose childish laughter I still hear when sleep doth cloy my brain. So gay, so young as I remember her. Whose innocent tears did make her eyes blue pools whose deeps uncharted hid what wonders none might guess at. The blood pounds in my brain and hurts my eyes. What would she say now to know her father was a murderer? She must never know, never behold my face. Yet I must see her once 'ere she departs. I must. I must. Yes, I'll have him bring her here that I may once again behold her face. It is impossible that she should remember me. The Beadle coming here—hm, that's good. For I'll dispose of him some way. Johanna safe, good, good. Then all that's left is that same Judge whom I so foolishly let slip. Then to the sea with Mrs Lovett? Hm, perhaps, perhaps. (*He is about to go when an idea suddenly strikes him*) Ah! The way is clear to end it all! These single threads begin to weave a pattern in my mind. Johanna free, brought hither by the sailor—that baits the hook will draw the Judge to me. And once drawn in—why then I'll gut him sure.

A Voice (*off, in a Devon accent*) Some service, Master Barber—are you there?

Todd That accent has a pleasant ring. (*He goes to the door*) Ascend, sir, if you please. I'll be with you straight. I'll soon polish him off!

Todd exits

SCENE 5

The Cellar

Mrs Lovett enters with Tobias

Mrs Lovett The ovens is over here. (*She crosses and opens the oven door*)

A red glow illuminates the stage

And make sure you close the door properly, like this. (*She closes the oven door*)

Tobias Cor, they're big enough, ain't they?

Mrs Lovett Scarce big enough to bake all the pies we sell. Ten dozen at a time, I do, but I ain't never got many over I can tell you. Now then, the meat deliveries are irregular, but I dare say you'll get the hang of it as you go along. The pies is down here—(*she goes off*)—and you can have as many as you fancy.

Tobias Now you're talking.

Mrs Lovett (*returning*) And here's a couple to be going on with.

Tobias Cor, ta.

Mrs Lovett Any questions?

Tobias No, not really, except that it's a bit nifty down here, i'n't it? Smells like something's died, or summat.

Mrs Lovett A rat, perhaps. I'll tell Mr Todd to see to it.

Tobias Well, it must have died of something pretty 'orrible to stink like it does. Cor dear!

Mrs Lovett I expect you'll get used to it.

Tobias Oh, don't worry—I can get used to anything.

Mrs Lovett I'll leave you, then.

Mrs Lovett exits

Tobias Cor dear, I ain't never smelt nothing like it. Oh well. (*He holds his nose with one hand and takes a bite out of the pie*) Mmmmmmm. That's better. A bit of all right, this is. (*Looking round*) These cellars aren't half big. Flaming huge, they are. I bet you can get yourself lost down there, unless you follow your nose. Never mind. (*He munches happily*) Hey, what's this? A hair! (*He finds a long hair in the pie*) Ycccc. That ain't very tasty, is it? (*He winds the hair round his finger*) Don't look like one of Mrs L's. Oh well, must have been a hairy cow, or something. Don't know that I fancy that one no more, though. (*He pushes the pie aside, takes another one and inspects it*) Yea, that's a good 'un. (*He bites into it*) Smashing! (*He chews ecstatically*) Aaaw! What's that? Come here, you little bleeder. Must be a bone or something. Funny shape for a bone. Here, it's a finger-nail—it's a whole bleedin' finger-nail. I don't think I like these pies no more.

There is a thump off

Whass that? (*He tiptoes off in the direction of the thump*) Aaaah! (*He returns, trembling*) A bloke with his head half sawed off. Oh Gawd, I'm getting out of here.

Tobias rushes off in the direction Mrs Lovett went. There is a banging off, then he returns

Locked. I can't get out! Help! Heeeelp! (*No answer*) Oh Gawd, oh, there must be another way out of here.

He rushes off

(*As he goes*) There must be, there must be, there must be . . .

SCENE 6

The Pie Shop

Mrs Lovett is rolling out pastry. Sweeney Todd enters

Todd Another one below.
Mrs Lovett I can hardly keep up with you. The lad'll know by now, then.
Todd That matters not. There's no way out beside the door. You locked it?
Mrs Lovett 'Course. What d'you take me for?
Todd Good. I didn't mean to criticize my love. And before the day is out it may be that your guest house by the sea has come a little nearer.
Mrs Lovett How d'yer mean?
Todd The Beadle's coming hither to investigate the smell arising from the cellar.
Mrs Lovett Is he, now . . .
Todd And before long perhaps he'll add to it.

A whistling is heard off

That sounds like Anthony. I must talk with him.

Todd exits

Mrs Lovett (*rolling industriously*) Won't be long now, and then I'll have him. All to meself. Oooooh. There we'll sit—wigglin' our toes in the sand. (*She sings an off-key version of Johanna's song*) Now where have I heard that? Oh, it's that sailor he's got upstairs, he's always humming it. (*She continues to sing*)

The Beadle enters behind her and coughs to attract her attention

Oh, Lord, and he i'n't here. (*Aloud*) Er—do come in, sir.
Beadle I'm in already.
Mrs Lovett So you are. Well, sit you down . . .
Beadle I'm here on official business, ma'am. There've been complaints . . .
Mrs Lovett About the smell? Oh, I know, it's shocking, i'n't it? Must be the rats or summat. Oh, you do look tired, must be this hot weather we're having. Why don't you take the weight off your feet a minute? Sit you down.
Beadle I'm a busy man, ma'am, and I'll thank you to let me inspect your cellar.
Mrs Lovett Oh, er—the keys are lost, sir. That's half the trouble, we can't get down there to find out what the trouble is.
Beadle (*making for the exit*) Then I'll have to break the door down, won't ı?
Mrs Lovett No!
Beadle And why not, pray? Is there something down there you don't want me to see?
Mrs Lovett No, no, it's just that them stairs is awful steep and I wouldn't want you to miss your step and do yourself a mischief nor nothing. Just let me set the table for Mr Todd and put his pie out for him. It's special for him, and I wouldn't want him to miss it and take an ordinary one by mistake. Ooooh, done to a turn, it is. (*She fetches the special pie and sniffs at it appreciatively*) Just how he likes it.
Beadle Between you and me, missus, I wouldn't bother setting the table; he won't be eating that pie of yours today.
Mrs Lovett Why ever not?
Beadle (*drawing a pistol and laying it on the table*) 'Cos when I've had a look down your cellars I'm going to arrest him.
Mrs Lovett Why? Arrest him! Whatever for?
Beadle I dunno. I'll have to think of something, but the Bishop was down this way to do a wedding yesterday, and he was so upset by the stink he damn near married the wrong people. Now, that won't do. He's complained to my superiors, and they want results. So take your pick. I've either got to arrest you or Mr Sweeney Todd. But first I'll have a look in that cellar and see just what's going on—then maybe I won't have to make up no charges against him. Maybe there'll be some real ones.
Mrs Lovett (*picking up the pie*) Oh, what a waste. I'll have to throw it

away now. (*She goes as if to throw the pie away*) I made it specially—slaved over it. It'd break my heart to see someone who didn't really appreciate it gobble it down. (*As if an idea has suddenly struck her*) Oooh, you wouldn't do me a favour, would you?

Beadle Madam, I'm a busy man. I've no time for favours.

Mrs Lovett (*languishing*) Oh, sir, and you look such a kind-hearted, considerate sort of man . . .

Beadle Oh, very well—what is it?

Mrs Lovett Would you eat it for me? Just so I know I haven't wasted all me labour. Would yer? Just to please a poor old widow?

Beadle Oh, very well. Give it here.

Mrs Lovett (*busily laying a place for him*) Ooooh, you've no idea the good things that's in there—only the juciest cuts of meat, and I stewed it ever so gently. There we are.

The Beadle tastes the pie

'Nough salt?

The Beadle has his mouth full, but indicates that there is

'Course, you can't really get the full flavour of it without a glass of ale to set it off. Shall I get you one—just to help it down, eh?

The Beadle's mouth is full again, but he nods vigorously. Mrs Lovett goes and pours a glass of ale

There, that'll do the trick. (*She puts poison in it. Aside*) And so it will, that's poison enough for twenty men. (*Aloud*) There you are. Good health, sir.

Beadle (*raising his glass to her*) Where's yours? (*He is about to drink, but stops*) Will you not join me in a glass?

Mrs Lovett Er—not now, not now.

Beadle (*putting the glass down in front of her*) Come, keep me company. I'll draw another for myself. (*He goes to pour another glass*)

Sweeney Todd enters

Mrs Lovett indicates the pistol and the Beadle, and indicates to him to get out. Instead, he hides. The Beadle returns with a glass of ale

Now, your health. (*He drinks and settles down to the pie again*)

Mrs Lovett (*painstakingly for Todd's benefit*) So stupid of me to lose the key of the cellar so you've got to break the door down.

Mrs Lovett looks enquiringly at Sweeney Todd, who thinks for a moment and then mimes having the key himself. Mrs Lovett queries this, but Todd is adamant

That Mr Todd's a fool. He's got no more brains than what's in that pie you're eating. No, I tell a lie—he's got less brains than there is in that pie. I'm not sorry you're going to arrest him——

Mrs Lovett looks at Sweeney Todd, who mimes "Continue"

—and I have my suspicions that he's the one who's got the key to the cellar——

Beadle A-ha.

Mrs Lovett —though what he wants it for is beyond me.

Sweeney Todd mimes various nefarious activities. Mrs Lovett mouths, "Have you gone mad?" The Beadle looks up and sees her

Beadle What's the matter, ma'am?

Mrs Lovett Oh—indigestion—er—it's all that worry I'm having about this cellar of mine and what Mr Todd does down there.

Beadle (*finishing the last of the pie and picking up his pistol*) Well, you won't need to be afraid of him much longer, ma'am. (*Rising*) Where is he?

Mrs Lovett Upstairs.

The Beadle moves away from the table. Mrs Lovett switches the ale glasses on him, and mimes "Poison" to Sweeney Todd, who nods appreciatively

Good health.

Beadle (*about to drink the poisoned one*) Oh, no, dear lady, this is your glass. See, it's nearly full. (*He switches the glasses back again and finishes off his own*)

Todd mimes "Go to the cellar"

My compliments. I've never tasted a better pie. And now I think I'll pay a call on Mr Todd before I see the cellars. If he has the key I can save myself the task of breaking down the door. Upstairs, you say?

Mrs Lovett nods

I will inform you of our interview.

The Beadle goes

Mrs Lovett Go to the cellar, he says. And what about the boy? (*She picks up a cleaver*) I s'pose I'd better do him if he interferes. All I ever wanted was a nice little house by the sea and enough to keep me comfy. And now look at me. My poor old Mum must be turning in her grave. Never mind, Mum, it's worth it to get some of that sea air in me lungs. And with him out of the way, we're half-way there.

Mrs Lovett exits

Scene 7

The Barber Shop

Sweeney Todd is pacing up and down

Todd I must not underestimate this man. He's tricked my Lucy to her downfall, he must not trick me. He'll not be shaved, that's sure, and yet . . . I hear him coming. (*He sits in his chair*)

The Beadle enters

Todd jumps up guiltily

Beadle Mr Todd.
Todd Sir.
Beadle What were you doing there?
Todd There? Where?
Beadle As you were sitting.
Todd Er—nothing—nothing at all.
Beadle Come, come, don't trifle with me. What were you about?
Todd Just sitting, waiting for a customer.
Beadle Hm. Let me see this chair.
Todd No. Stand back.
Beadle (*levelling his pistol at Todd*) Out of the way. I'll see it. (*He examines the chair*)
Todd No! Don't sit!
Beadle And why not?
Todd It—er—it may be dangerous.
Beadle Dangerous? Not while I have my pistol, Mr Todd. (*He sits*) There, see now, I am still quite safe. Now, what is there about this chair that makes you so afraid?
Todd I am discovered. My guilt is found. Oh, sir, have mercy on me. I will share it all with you if you let me go free.
Beadle Share what?
Todd My guilty spoils. There is a lever that operates a secret drawer, and in it are my jewels, for I have sometime been a thief.
Beadle Your jewels, eh?
Todd Rubies and pearls, great emeralds and diamonds—enough for both of us.
Beadle I think not, Mr Todd. Enough for me alone, perhaps. Why should I share with a thief? If I but pull this trigger, all is mine. But first, let's see this treasure.

Todd works the mechanism and the Beadle disappears with a scream

Todd The treasure is all yours, my friend. I wish you joy of it! (*He calls down into the cellar*) Mrs Lovett, all is well, I trust?
Mrs Lovett (*below*) All's well, his neck is broken.

Todd Dispose of him. No trouble from the boy?
Mrs Lovett I don't know where he is.
Todd Seeking another exit from the prison—he'll find no comfort there. (*He goes to the door*) The end's in sight—one more and we'll be done. Now I must write a letter to the Judge to lure him hither and complete the score. I'll do it straight. Oh, haste the night!

Todd exits

SCENE 8

A Room in the Lunatic Asylum

Anthony is discovered in disguise and carrying a bundle

Anthony So far, all's well. What kind of man's this Jonas Fogg that he immures so many souls within these high and flinty walls? I'll not hesitate to kill a man like him. Soft, he comes—and Johanna's with him!

Jonas Fogg enters, leading Johanna. Her hands are tied

Fogg Ah, Mr—Quilt. Your servant. (*He proffers his hand*)
Anthony (*aside*) I'll not shake hands with such a man. And yet I must. (*Aloud, shaking Fogg's hand*) You do me honour, Mr Fogg. Have you perused my letter?

At the sound of Anthony's voice Johanna looks up

Fogg I have indeed, and I agree it would be to our mutual interest to come to some agreement in regard of my poor children's hair.
Anthony Your—children?
Fogg We are one happy family here, sir, and all my patients are my children, to be corrected when they're naughty, and rewarded with a sweetie when they're good. But to our business. This daughter here has hair the shade you mentioned in your notice. Poor child, she needs so much correction, she sings if left alone. Come, child, smile for this gentleman and you shall have a sweetie.
Anthony (*aside*) Oh, friend!
Fogg I shall correct you if you do not smile.
Anthony (*quickly*) This woman looks not mad.
Fogg Alas, she is. As mad as you or I.
Anthony What do you mean?
Fogg Why, who is maddest—he who's shut away or he who puts him there? What more unnatural act is there to deny a fellow creature air and light? And yet a dozen times a day the father shuts away the daughter, or the son the mother. Shuts them away from sunlight, friends and daily intercourse—why, sir, it is the act of a cruel and desperate lunatic.

Anthony But you—you preside over this place . . .

Fogg And therefore it is fitting that I should be the maddest man in here. What else can you expect in a world as mad as this? Why, only look at your own trade, sir. Do you not think it is exceedingly odd practice to shave off all one's hair and then pay someone like you to knit one a hat out of somebody else's? And all for nothing. Look, look here. (*He removes a skull from under his cloak*) How would this stern unbending matron look in a wig? Would a ribboned bonnet grace this brow? Can painting make these cheeks more comely? Or a patch make dimples in this chin? Yet in her life she did all that and more, whilst children starved and age crept into cold and cheerless hovels. And all for what? For this? Oh, surely she was mad, for if she'd looked into her mirror with a candid eye, then this is what she would have seen. And this is what we all will see—deny it how we may. 'Tis madness to think otherwise. And now to business. (*He removes a pair of shears from under his cloak*) Stand still, my child, and you shall have a sweetie.

Anthony (*drawing a pistol*) Stay your hand.

Fogg You see, you're mad to think a madman like myself would be deterred by such a thing as that. Now, where shall I cut?

Anthony Stop, or I fire.

Fogg Fire, and I will stop.

Anthony I cannot shoot. (*He drops the pistol and rushes over to restrain Fogg*)

Fogg throws Johanna to the ground and turns on Anthony, who backs away. Fogg follows him. Johanna picks up the pistol

Fogg And you are mad to drop your pistol, sir, for now I'll clip your neck.

Anthony trips and falls. Fogg is about to stab him, when Johanna shoots him in the back

Now do you see my skull? Was I not right? (*He dies*)

Johanna bursts into tears. Anthony goes to her

Anthony Comfort, my love. Let me untie your hands. (*He does so*) And then we will away. Have courage, sweet, for we shall soon be married, and then to my ship and leave this evil town a hundred leagues behind. I have brought clothes that you may come away quite undetected. (*He unpacks his bundle*) They should rightly fit upon a manly form, but they will serve our purpose well.

Johanna unwraps the clothes. Anthony takes a bunch of keys from Fogg's pocket

The friend who planned this enterprise awaits us, we must call on him before we join my ship. And now, my love, let us away. (*He unlocks the door*)

Johanna and Anthony exit

SCENE 9

The Judge's House

The Judge is discovered reading a letter

Judge (*reading*) "I make thus bold to write to your Honour because at our first parting you were angry with me, and I would not have incurred your Honour's wrath for anything. That foolish sailor whom you chanced to meet at my poor shop was, I assure you, no friend of mine—and I hope that the information that I am able to lay before you will allay any suspicions you have. Your daughter Johanna has been abducted from the institution where you wisely placed her, by that same rash, impudent fellow, and they plan to board his ship this very night. But I have managed by a subterfuge to persuade him to bring her to my shop in Fleet Street before they embark. If you would apprehend them, come at once, and I will assist you in returning your ward to you. I beg you to come alone, as the sailor is already half mad, and may do her some mischief if he suspects he has been discovered. But I am sure that together we can outwit him: he still has a misplaced trust in me, and that will serve our purpose well. I am, sir, your most obedient servant and well-wisher, Sweeney Todd." Escaped! It cannot be—but if I find it so, then that same foolish sailor shall dangle from a rope before the week is out. I'll straight to Jonas Fogg, and if this news be confirmed I'll follow Mr Todd's directions. Oh, a worthy man—I have misjudged h. m sure.

The Judge exits

SCENE 10

The Barber Shop

Johanna enters, disguised as a boy, with Anthony

Johanna Why must we wait? I fear that this delay will hurt our purpose.
Anthony He promised he'd bestow his blessing on us, and I would not leave without it. Why, it is he who saved you from that hellish place.
Johanna I must seem ungrateful—but I fear. Where is your friend, where is he? Surely he must know the danger we're in.
Anthony He will be here, I promise. But I think I saw Mrs Lovett enter an alehouse further down the street. I'll go to seek her. She may have news of Sweeney Todd.
Johanna Oh, do not leave me alone. I am afraid. There was an old beggar woman by the door below, who stared at us as we came in. I fear she means us harm.

Anthony No, 'tis me she stared at, for she knows me well and wonders at my clothes. I'll reassure her before I go to seek good Mrs Lovett. Have no fear.

Johanna But yet I do.

Anthony (*seating her in a chair*) I'll wager you will be as safe here as on my ship. I'll not be long. Think of the future—that will raise your spirits.

Johanna I will—and see, already do I smile.

Anthony exits

But yet I'll not feel safe 'till water's parted us from England. (*She goes to the window and looks out*) Where is this Sweeney Todd? Would he would come. Ha! Someone approaches—perhaps . . . No, 'tis that beggar woman. Oh! She suspects. I needs must hide myself. (*She gets into the chest and closes the lid*)

The Beggar Woman enters

Beggar Woman The sailor's gone and left his young companion hereabouts. I must warn him. (*She looks around*) Not here? Boy? Where are you?

The Beggar Woman exits down the back stairs
Sweeney Todd enters

Todd So, it is done. All's well again. The letter is delivered and Judge Turpin's gone to Jonas Fogg—alone. And he will soon be here. I must prepare.

The Beggar Woman enters

(*Aside*) The foolish beggar woman. Curse her, she'll mar all. She must die. (*He creeps up behind the Beggar Woman, stifles her cries with a hand across her face, and cuts her throat. He then manhandles her into the chair. He is about to work the mechanism, when he thinks better of it*) No, she will serve to make the trick still sweeter. 'Tis dark enough, and with her head thus forward he will not see her face. Now, Judge, the time draws nigh when justice will be done. (*He goes to the window and looks out*)

Johanna cautiously raises the lid of the chest and sees the Beggar Woman

Johanna (*aside*) Oh, no, she sits and waits! Pray God that Anthony is safe. (*She lowers the lid again*)

Todd 'Tis he. 'Tis he! And alone—hurrying blindly to his lawful end.

Footsteps are heard and the Judge enters warily

Judge Mr Todd?

Todd (*whispering*) Here, your Honour. Sssh! She is asleep.

Judge Asleep?

Todd In the chair.

Judge What of the sailor?

Todd Also asleep, but he is in the cellar, never to leave there if it please your Honour. I gave them both a cunning draft mixed in a cup of wine, and now await your pleasure.

Judge Oh, excellent barber, how I have misjudged you! But that looks not like my poor Johanna's form . . .

Todd The sailor forced her to disguise herself as a poor beggar woman that they might slip away from London undetected.

Judge You say he forced her?

Todd It was strange, but she seemed loth to look upon his face. She is much changed, more humble in her manner, and I think, if he'd not forced her to elope with him, she would have done your pleasure.

Judge What?

Todd She spoke of you as sleep closed on her eyes, and murmured of your kindness, which she, fond virgin, had mistook the while. Old Jonas Fogg's correction haply did some good.

Judge Oh, let me wake her and confirm this news!

Todd Ssh! Softly, softly, it is not well to wake her so roughly from so deep a sleep, so gently, gently; wake her with a kiss.

Judge Oh, happy man! (*He approaches the Beggar Woman*) Johanna? Daughter, soon to be my wife, your husband calls . . . (*He goes to kiss her*) Aaaagh! What's this?

Todd (*whipping round between the Judge and the door*) A wife more fitting for you. You may marry her in hell. (*He works the chair and the Beggar Woman drops*)

Judge But my Johanna . . .

Todd That was not her, but some deluded hag who chanced along. What, do you think that I'll play pander to my own dear daughter?

Judge (*backing away*) Daughter?

Todd Aye, that was my word. I told you once before you tried a case concerned my wife. Her name was Lucy, and a sweeter maid ne'er graced the cobbles with her dainty tread. Myself, a humble barber, was no match for you, armed with the heavy sword of law. (*He flicks open a razor*) But now we're matched more even.

Todd drives the Judge backwards until he tumbles and sits in the chair

Judge No, no . . .

Todd kills the Judge

Todd Now, Judge, your soul is licked in flame already—let your body follow it. (*He works the chair*) 'Tis done. And fairly done. Now murder shall melt from my heart as frost before the sun. (*To the razor*) Oh, true and honest friend, your thirst is slaked at last—now sleep the sleep of angels, undisturbed. (*He closes the razor and puts it down. Calling*) Mrs Lovett? Are you there? The Judge is down below. Let him but follow the Beadle and our work is done.

Mrs Lovett (*off*) I'll see to it. I've just this minute got in. The sailor's been asking for you, so I sent him on a wild goose chase up St Dunstan's.
Todd (*aside*) Anthony. They must have come and found me out. (*To Mrs Lovett*) It is no matter. Attend the cellar. (*Aside*) I must go and look for him. Now that my vengeance is assuaged I long to see Johanna.

Todd exits

There is a pause, then Johanna emerges cautiously from the chest

Johanna All gone at last, thank God. What work was here? I heard several voices but could make nothing out distinctly. Now I'll stay no longer, but seek Anthony.

Sweeney Todd enters

Todd (*aside*) No, I'll wait here. He surely will return and I might miss him on the way. (*He sees Johanna*) Whence comes this boy? None passed me on the stairs. Has he been here concealed the while? (*Aloud*) What is your business? How long have you been here? Speak quickly.
Johanna (*aside*) This must be the barber—yet he frightens me, he looks not like a man to trust.
Todd Come, speak. What would you?
Johanna Is this not a barber's shop?
Todd It is.
Johanna Then may not a man seek service here?
Todd Indeed he may, sir. Do but sit. (*Aside, as he fetches the razor*) Must murder rise again? Here's yet another must complete the score.
Johanna I cannot stay, sir. I have urgent business. (*She rises*)
Todd (*pushing her down again*) But sit, sir! (*Aside*) He forces me to hurry, and I will. (*Aloud*) If you would but tip back your head . . .

Johanna does so

(*Aside*) 'Tis sure he did not come here for a shave, there's not a hair upon his chin. Then why came he? To hinder me, 'tis sure. He must die —now, this instant.

Sweeney Todd is on the point of cutting Johanna's throat when there is a terrible scream from Mrs Lovett below. Todd starts back

What noise was that? Perhaps the Judge still lives, or that brat has done her harm. I must find out.

Todd rushes out, razor in hand

Johanna (*rising*) What hellish cry was that? Oh, now I'll run, for see—the way is clear.

Johanna runs off

SCENE 11

The Cellar

*Mrs Lovett enters, dragging the body of the Beggar Woman towards the
oven*

Mrs Lovett The flesh must fry, the bones turn to ash, and then we will
away. So close, so close! I've waited all this time, and now the guest
house is within my grasp. No-one shall take it from me. Quickly,
quickly.

Todd rushes in

Todd Why did you scream? The Judge, does he still live?
Mrs Lovett No, no. It—was the boy—jumped out on me. But now he's
run off. It's me nerves, I'm sorry. It was just nerves.
Todd Your nerves may rest in peace, the last is done. The flames will hide
our secret. Here, let me help you. (*He goes to assist Mrs Lovett with the
Beggar Woman*)
Mrs Lovett No! Leave her be.
Todd Why, what's the matter? You are not well, my dear. Rest awhile,
I will dispose of her.
Mrs Lovett You shall not! No, you shall not.
Todd Something's amiss. Here, let me see her face.
Mrs Lovett No, no . . .

*Todd pushes her away and examines the face of the Beggar Woman by the
light of the oven*

Todd It is impossible! Tell me the light is false, or that I dream. Woman,
is not this cold and lifeless form the body of my dear wife, Lucy?
Your silence is an answer in itself. Ah, Lucy! (*He buries his head on her
breast, sobbing loudly*)
Mrs Lovett I lied because I loved you, Mr Todd. What chance had I got
if she was still alive? I knew you'd seek her out. But she wouldn't have
done all them things I've done for you, would she? Just give me a chance
and I'll be twice the wife she was to you. Please, Mr Todd, please . . .
Todd (*rising slowly and covering the body*) Life is for the living, Mrs
Lovett, and I have grieved for her already.
Mrs Lovett You mean it? You're not angry with me? You'll still marry
me and we can go to the seaside?
Todd Of course my love.

*Mrs Lovett goes to him and they kiss. Todd manœuvres her gently towards
the oven*

Mrs Lovett What are you . . . ?

Todd pushes her into the oven. She screams

Todd Lie there and take the devil for a mate—false, perjured hag! (*Turning back to Lucy's body*) But oh, the wheel has come full circle. (*He takes out the razor*) This blade has sliced through flesh of my flesh, stained my hands with blood as dear to me as that which surges from my own black heart. (*He hurls the razor away and kneels beside the body*) Oh, Lucy, Lucy! (*He takes her in his arms and weeps*)

Tobias is heard singing "Simple Simon" as he approaches

The boy. Oh, now I do repent, and I will set him free. It matters not that he informs the world of all our dreadful deeds. (*Calling*) Tobias! Come hither to me. Come! Don't be afraid.

Tobias enters slowly. His hair has turned completely white. He is quite mad

Tobias Pat-a-cake, pat-a-cake, baker's man; Bake me a cake . . . No—no, no, no, no, no. It's pies! Bake me a pie, to delight my eye, and I will—sigh if the crust—be high. (*He laughs insanely*)

Todd Tobias, you are free. Look, the door is open. I'll not stop you.

Tobias (*seeing the Beggar Woman*) Ah! I gave her a ha'penny and she told me they weren't tasty. (*He laughs, then sings*)

> Sing a song of ha'penny,
> A pocket full of rye,
> Four-and-twenty dead men
> Baked in a pie.
> When the pie was opened
> The men began to sing—

Wasn't that a dainty dish to set before a boy who never did no-one no harm in all his life.

Todd (*gently*) Tobias, you are free.

Tobias (*grabbing the body and shaking her violently*) Not tasty! Not tasty! Not tasty!

Todd Leave her in peace. (*He flings Tobias away*) You shall not harm her, no! (*He cradles the body again*)

Tobias finds the razor. He examines it and plays with it

Tobias Razor! Razor, razor, razor, razor! Cut, cut, cudougan, watch me grind my corn! (*He starts to cut at Sweeney Todd*) Pat him, and prick him, and mark him with B, and put him in the oven for baby and me! (*He cuts Todd's throat*)

Todd dies across the body of Lucy. The sound of people approaching is heard

No, no!

Tobias runs off.
Anthony, Johanna and the Officers of the Watch enter

Johanna The scream was from below. This should be the place.

The Officers search the cellars

Anthony (*seeing Todd*) Oh, my friend! What murderous angel visited here and did such bloody work?
Watch (*off*) And here's another. Why it's—Judge Turpin.
Johanna My guardian? Dead?

The Watch enters

Watch Quite dead.

Tobias runs on

Tobias (*to the Watch, who is investigating the bodies*) Keep off! They're mine, mine!
Watch What are?
Tobias The pies, the pies! They're mine!
Watch I'll not steal them.
Tobias No! No, you shall not, for what I have to tell will, I fear, quite spoil your appetite. Mrs Lovett's pies are made from human flesh. (*He takes a hand from inside his shirt*) Look! (*He laughs and starts to eat*)
Anthony (*turning away*) The boy's mad.
Watch And dangerous, too. Boy, come with us.
Tobias No, I have work to do. I must mince this meat. (*He indicates Todd and Lucy*)
Anthony Take him away.
Watch We will, sir. And question him to find the truth of this.

The Watch exit with Tobias

Anthony (*to Todd's lifeless body*) My friend, we stayed that you might bless our union. Alas, that now you cannot. (*To Johanna*) My love, the Judge is dead, nothing now stands between us. Let's be married straight, then aboard my ship, and leave this evil town far, far behind us.
Johanna With all my heart. Oh, let us go.

Johanna and Anthony exit, as

the CURTAIN *falls*

FURNITURE AND PROPERTY LIST

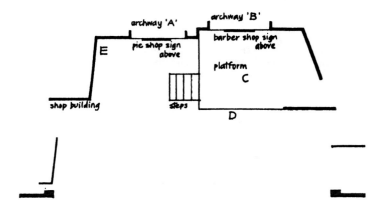

ACT I

SCENE 1

On stage: Street light. Drop shop frontage over archways "A" and "B"
Pie shop sign

SCENE 2

Strike: Street lamp and shop frontage at archway "A"

Set: Counter and shelves in front of archway "A". *On them:* plates, cutlery, tray, pie dishes with pies, jug of ale, tankards, glasses, pots of seasonings, razors in box
Table
2 chairs

DUMB SHOW

Set: Candelabra (set by dancers)
Revolve counter to show bookshelves

DUMB SHOW ENDS

Set: Pie shop as before

SCENE 3

Strike: Pie shop props

Set: Street cross and sign in centre of platform "C"
Street backing in arches "A" and "B"
Chairs placed down R and down L of platform

SCENE 4

Strike: Market-place props
Window in arch

Set: Ornate chair. Balustrade at front of platform "C"
Couch at "D". French windows at archway "A"
Doorway in archway "B". Chandelier down R of platform

SCENE 5

Strike: Judge's house props

Set: Large chest at "D"
Barber shop sign
Pegs on wall
2 chairs—one in centre of platform "C"
Table. *On it:* various shaving implements in box, towels

SCENE 6

Strike: Barber shop props

Set: Judge's house props

SCENE 7

Strike: Judge's house props

Set: Court seat with royal cypher at "D"
Asylum gates at archway "A"

SCENE 8

Strike: Courtroom props

Set: Barber shop props

DUMB SHOW

Set: Asylum barred gates in arch. Strike at end of tableau

Off stage: Lighting pole (Lamplighter)
Bowl (Beggar Woman)
Bottle of Elixir (Tobias)
2 high-backed chairs with strops attached (Tobias)
Razor (Alfredo)
Shaving soap, brush, bowl (Todd)
Forceps (Alfredo)
Forceps (Todd)
Bible (Judge)
Scourge (Judge)
Mop and duster (Mrs Lovett)
Black cap (Beadle)

Personal: Anthony: coins
Alfredo: coins, notes
Johanna: ring

ACT II

SCENE 1

On stage: Street lamp, pie shop sign as Act I, Scene 1

SCENE 2

Strike: Street lamp

Set: Barber shop props, with special trick chair on platform in addition
Shop generally tidier and smarter than before
Asylum gates at archway "A"

SCENE 3

Set: Archway over platform "C" hiding barber's chair

SCENE 4

Strike: Asylum gates

Set: Pie shop props
On table: chopping board, pastry, meat, bowl, knife
On dresser: fresh dish of pies

SCENE 5

Strike: Pie shop props

Set: Ovens at "E"

SCENE 6

Strike: Ovens

Set: Pie shop props
            On table: pastry, with roller and board, cleaver
            On dresser: special pie with plate, knife and fork, poison bottle

SCENE 7

Strike: Pie shop props

Set: Barber shop props

SCENE 8

Strike: Barber shop props

Set: Asylum gates (from inside) and chair in front of them
            Archway over platform "C"

SCENE 9

Strike: Asylum gates

Set: Judge's house props

SCENE 10

Strike: Judge's house props. Archway over platform "C"

Set: Barber shop props

SCENE 11

Strike: Barber shop props

Set: Ovens at "E". Chest at "D". Archway on platform "C"

Off stage: Tray of pies (Tobias)
            Pistol (Anthony)
            Pies (Mrs Lovett)
            Pistol (Beadle)
            Bundle of clothing (Anthony)
            Rope (to tie Johanna's hands)
            Skull (Fogg)
            Shears (Fogg)
            Open letter (Judge)
            Severed hand (Tobias)

Personal: Fogg: bunch of keys

LIGHTING PLOT

Property fittings required: nil
Standing set—interior and exterior

ACT I

To open: Dim night street lighting

Cue 1	At end of Scene 1 *Cross-fade to pie shop lighting*	(Page 2)
Cue 2	At end of Scene 2 *Cross-fade to street lighting, day*	(Page 6)
Cue 3	At end of Scene 3 *Cross-fade to Judge's house lighting*	(Page 10)
Cue 4	At end of Scene 4 *Cross-fade to Barber shop lighting*	(Page 12)
Cue 5	At end of Scene 5 *Cross-fade to Judge's house lighting*	(Page 16)
Cue 6	At end of Scene 6 *Cross-fade to Court Room lighting*	(Page 17)
Cue 7	At end of Scene 7 *Cross-fade to Barber shop lighting*	(Page 18)

ACT II

To open: Street lighting, day

Cue 8	At end of Scene 1 *Cross-fade to Barber shop lighting*	(Page 24)
Cue 9	At end of Scene 2 *Cross-fade to Asylum gates, dull daylight*	(Page 26)
Cue 10	At end of Scene 3 *Cross-fade to Pie shop lighting*	(Page 28)
Cue 11	At end of Scene 4 *Cross-fade to dim cellar light*	(Page 32)
Cue 12	Mrs Lovett opens oven doors *Suffuse stage with red glow—fade as she closes oven doors*	(Page 32)
Cue 13	At end of Scene 5 *Cross-fade to Pie shop lighting*	(Page 33)

Cue 14	At end of Scene 6 *Cross-fade to Barber shop lighting*	(Page 36)
Cue 15	At end of Scene 7 *Cross-fade to Asylum interior lighting*	(Page 38)
Cue 16	At end of Scene 8 *Cross-fade to Judge's house lighting*	(Page 39)
Cue 17	At end of Scene 9 *Cross-fade to Barber shop lighting*	(Page 40)
Cue 18	At end of Scene 10 *Cross-fade to Cellar lighting, with red glow from ovens*	(Page 43)

EFFECTS PLOT

ACT I

Cue 1   At start of Scene 6   **(Page 16)**
            Clock chimes

Cue 2   **Johanna:** ... "I fear the worst."   **(Page 16)**
            Sound of stone hitting glass

ACT II

Cue 3   At start of Scene 3   **(Page 27)**
            Bell tolls, continue for a few lines into dialogue